Staffing your Children's Ministry

VERNIE SCHORR & WES HAYSTEAD

STANDARD PUBLISHING™

Cincinnati, Ohio

This volume is dedicated with deep affection to my children, Diane Sanders and Steve Schorr. They are the first children God gave me to win, train, and disciple for Christ. As adults they are my support, inspiration, and encouragement.

It is also dedicated with appreciation and love to all those who enabled and trained me and to those who served with me as volunteers. They are truly the authors of many of the concepts in this book.

A special note of appreciation to Toni Baldwin, who spent hours in conversation, editing, and encouragement.

And above all, acknowledgment to our great God and Savior Jesus for his wisdom, guidance, tender mercy, and unbounded grace.

This revised edition incorporates ideas and suggestions from children's leaders who have been helped by the concepts and strategies presented in this manual. As time goes by, the principles and objectives remain the same in ministering to children, but the specific approaches are adapted to fit new circumstances.

Staffing Your Children's Ministry
© 1991 and 1999 Standard Publishing
A division of Standex International Corporation
© 1999 by Vernie Schorr
All rights reserved
Printed in the United States of America

Credits
Cover and inside design: Liz Howe
Inside illustrations: Liz Howe, Jan Knudson, Sam Thiewes
Editor: Patricia Alderdice Senseman
Acquisitions editor: Ruth Frederick

06 05 04 03 02 01 00 99   5 4 3 2 1

ISBN 0-7847-0948-3

Contents

The Value of Children's Ministry

The Process of Recruiting

The Long Term Solution

Training Sessions

The Need and the Vision

Barry was fearful of teaching children. Only after a one-on-one conversation with the children's director and a guarantee that this would not be a "life sentence" did he hesitantly commit to try teaching five-year-olds.

His first challenge was a boy named Eric. Two months of Eric's disruptive and aggressive behavior sent Barry back to the children's director asking, "What do I do now?"

"Continue to love him, and find out what is going on in the family" was Toni's wise counsel. Barry made a visit to Eric's home and discovered a single mother under stress over a recent divorce due to a history of abuse.

Barry began to pray for Eric and decided Eric needed a consistent and loving man in his life, and he began to spend time with Eric outside the classroom. He went to Eric's T-ball and soccer games, occasionally treated Eric and a friend to soft drinks, and with another teacher, took Eric and his classmates to the park. In class, Barry made sure that Eric received plenty of positive, encouraging attention.

At the end of the Sunday school year, Eric did not want to be promoted to first grade because he was afraid he would no longer see Barry. But Barry assured him that it was important to become a first grader. He promised Eric he would continue to be his friend and that he would still want to see Eric play ball.

That was four years ago. Barry continues to teach five-year-olds in Sunday school. He no longer fears teaching children; instead, he eagerly anticipates each opportunity to invest in their lives. You would not be able to get him out of the classroom with a cannonball. What a reward for both the children's director who recruited Barry and for Barry himself! And what a benefit for Eric and dozens of other children taught and loved by Barry!

What if Barry had not been asked because no one had seen what God could do through him? What if his initial reluctance had discouraged the children's director from prayerfully encouraging Barry to try? What if the approaches made to Barry had focused only on signing up someone to take a turn with those five-year-olds? Our attitudes as recruiters need to reflect the great reward of finding the best for one of the most influential ministries available to followers of Jesus Christ.

What an adventure to recruit people to meet the needs of children . . . to find those who will nurture a vision for the potential within children . . . to equip and train others to impart the values of love and trust to a child, to develop the very character of God in a child's life!

As people involved in recruiting teachers and others for children's ministry, we are never out of a job. The task is an ongoing and never-ending adventure in prayer and involvement with people. Expand your understanding of the need and renew your vision of recruitment: equipping loving adults to serve children. You can experience the reward of recruiting people to be a part of shaping and growing the future army of the kingdom of God!

NOTE: Some people dislike the term *recruiting*. To them the word conveys images of arm-twisting, pleading, even manipulating. They prefer to think of volunteers offering to serve. However, in the real world of ministry, there has always been a shortage of eager volunteers. Even Jesus lamented that "the workers are few" (Matthew 9:37). In this book, recruiting encompasses the reality that a great many people need a nudge, a challenge, in order to seriously consider the possibility that God has gifted them to be his hands in touching children's lives. The approaches suggested in these pages intentionally avoid applying pressure or seeking to make people feel guilty enough that they will agree to "take a turn." *Recruiting is the process of prayerfully linking people, sometimes even reluctant people, with ministry opportunities that can revolutionize their lives at the same time they minister to children.*

Examine the Need

The needs of children have never been greater, and the church has never been less prepared to meet these needs.

Read a church newsletter or bulletin during the summer months and you will notice these familiar words: "Wanted: Children's workers. Loving, caring, concerned, committed Christians."

No other time in our history has this statement been more valid than now. We need loving, caring, teachable adults to build positive relationships with children, to introduce them to God and his son, Jesus. We need people of high moral character to help children develop their awareness of God's character so that they want to grow towards him.

Because recruitment often is viewed as a distasteful job, it's easy to lose your perspective about the importance of placing adults in positions where they understand the need, catch the vision, and value the children they serve. But recruiting can be a rewarding and challenging part of ministry to children.

Scripture provides a strong foundation for the recruitment process. Jesus made it clear that the first step is to undergird the recruitment process with prayer. "Then He said to His disciples, 'The harvest is plentiful, but the workers are few. Therefore, beseech the Lord of the harvest to send out workers into His harvest'" (Matthew 9:37, 38). These words are as true today as when Jesus spoke them. Pray specifically for the people needed for your congregation's ministry to children. *You can then expect God to supply the workers!*

Step two is to remember the Source of all we think and say and do. Take a moment to read John 15. Abide in Christ. Seek out others who practice abiding in him and whose lives produce fruit. Share the wonderful opportunities to make a difference in the lives of children. Communicate this biblical directive as you share the opportunities for service. Children's ministry provides rich opportunities for the harvest that is the outgrowth of abiding in Christ.

Step three in the recruitment process is motivation. John 21:15-17 provides an example of motivation based on love. Jesus' conversation with Peter reinforces obedience based on love for Jesus and compassion for others. "Do you love me?" Jesus asked. Peter's answer was yes. Jesus' response was, "Tend my sheep." The privilege of

The
Need
and the
Vision

the recruiter is to enable Christians to tend his sheep through the vehicle of ministry to children.

Today's Child in Today's Culture

I was seated directly behind the driver of a school bus parked at the curb of a street in Brooklyn. Annie stumbled up the steps, screaming, "Leave me alone!" over her shoulder at her mother.

"You dummy, you can't even get on this ol' bus!" her mother screamed back. "You get home on time, and try to say something bright in school today!"

Annie turned her head and caught my eye. The smile she gave me did not communicate the emotional abuse she experiences each day. Her beautiful jacket and designer clothes denied the reality of the daily belittling that robs her of a sense of belonging and worth.

The next three children who boarded our bus wore thin sweaters. Their hair was uncombed. One had a bruise over her right eye, and another had a split lip. They said they had fallen down the stairs in their home. The situation would be reported, but little would be done because the caseloads were so great.

Where are the teachable, caring adults in these children's lives?

What a world children face today! Drug-addicted babies; split families; homelessness; homosexual parents; permissiveness in society; permissive parents; overindulgence; physical, emotional, and sexual abuse.

But depreciation and rejection are often more subtle.

One Christmas morning a mother, her five-year-old son, and her own mother entered a large church. They located the Sunday school class for five-year-olds and waited by the door expectantly. Four teachers were gathered in the center of a delightful room, busily talking about their Christmas plans.

"Good morning," said the mother.

"Merry Christmas," replied one of the teachers.

More waiting.

"Excuse me," said the mother. "Do we need a name tag for Geoff?"

There was no response.

"Mom, I don't think they want me here," Geoff said.

"Excuse me," said his mother again. "Is there something we need to do to register?"

"Look for his name tag on the counter," replied a teacher, quickly returning to her conversation.

"He doesn't have a name tag," said Geoff's mother. "We already looked. He hasn't been here since September."

"Well," said the teacher, "he must be in another class."

Only at the caring insistence of his mother and grandmother was Geoff finally registered and invited into the classroom.

Neglect comes in many forms. In a rural community in the Appalachian Mountains, a child hands his one-year-old sister a baby bottle filled with a soft drink.

"Henry, quit messin' with that baby and get off to school before I give you a good whoppin'!" yells his mother.

There is more of that soft drink sold in rural Perry County than in New York City.

Family values are created out of a sense of disregard and poverty. Meals are "fast food," served in front of TVs without consideration for nutrition or family bonding. Parents receive little or no help in child training. Much of the discipline is punitive, fracturing children's sense of belonging, worth, and competence.

The evidence of neglect and abuse in its many forms, at every level of our society, makes us wonder about our distorted appreciation of the gift and worth of children.

Today's Child in God's Eyes

Scripture repeatedly assigns great value to children. Psalm 127:3 says, "Behold, children are a gift of the LORD." In Deuteronomy 6, Moses commands the Israelites to instruct their children about God in everyday circumstances, with the purpose of raising children who will follow God's way and continue to tell others about him.

Jesus valued children. "'Let the little children come to me. Don't stop them. The kingdom of God belongs to people who are like these little children. I tell you the truth. You must accept the kingdom of God as a little child accepts things, or you will never enter it.' Then Jesus took the children in his arms. He put his hands on them and blessed them" (Mark 10:14-16, *ICB*). Jesus saw children as the heritage and hope of the kingdom of God.

Children are able to understand a great deal more of God's Word than adults often recognize. "From childhood you have known the sacred writings which are able to give you the wisdom that leads to salvation through faith which is in Christ Jesus" (2 Timothy 3:15). Can we do less than provide caring teachers of high moral character to share God's Word?

God desires that children be drawn to him as they learn of him. Children learn as they participate in well-planned and well-prepared learning experiences. They learn as they interact and build friendships with adults and other children. They learn as they observe the lives of the significant adults in their environment.

You, the recruiter, have the unique opportunity to influence the character and lives of both children and adults! You will influence and minister alongside adults as you enable adults to become an integral part of children's ministry. You will influence the lives of children as you recruit, train, and develop adults to participate in children's lives. You are truly blessed to be involved in the recruitment process!

Catch the Vision

The numbers of children to whom we minister are enormous. There are over 260 million people in the United States. Approximately fifty-seven million are children under the age of fourteen. Allow that figure to stagger your mind! Fifty-seven million children in the United States to be reached for Christ!

Recruiting can be an extremely rewarding experience! Recruiters are able to communicate the value of service and the joy that is available to those who serve. Develop a churchwide attitude that there is a place of service for everyone. Communicate positive aspects of children's ministry programs. Help church members discover their gifts, and encourage them to use those gifts.

The
Need
and the
Vision

Specific ways to accomplish these goals will be developed as you continue to read. Anticipate a successful recruitment program. You will be blessed as you enable adults to minister effectively to children!

Change Lives and Build Character

A vision for children's ministry must be built on awareness of needs to be accomplished in children's lives. In the limited time most people have to participate in a volunteer ministry, it is vital that time and energy is focused on truly important goals and objectives. From the first contact made to a prospective children's staff member, it should be made clear what is viewed as most essential.

Developing conscience and character in children ranks high in the list of responsibilities for any adult involved in the life of a child. In the past, building character in children was seen as the cooperative work of home, church, school, and government. As the child encountered the wider society, the same basic character virtues were taught and reinforced, helping children to choose right instead of wrong.

In recent years my own ministry to children has been a response to a radical shift that has occurred in many areas of our culture, surrounding children with destructive character traits and values systems. Even in early childhood, the media repeatedly exposes children to violence, anger, and revenge as the ways to solve conflicts. Many "heroes" and "heroines" of today are role models for selfishness, greed, and materialism. Fragmented families leave far too many children, even the affluent, searching for security and belonging, and finding it only in the brutal world of gangs and drugs and promiscuous sex.

Awareness of this shift obligated me to rethink how and what is being developed in the spirit, conscience, and mind of today's child. How can the pervasive negative influences on children be overcome? How can parents and volunteers make a positive difference? The need is not for "warm bodies" to run programs, but for committed people who will be intentional about developing children's conscience and character, helping them choose to grow toward God. Efforts to guide children to respond to God's love must include very practical guidance in how godly attitudes and actions grow out of a personal relationship with Jesus Christ. At the same time, loving, thoughtful encouragement towards godly living is a vital component in helping children come to faith in Christ.

Lives really are changed and positive character development occurs when the Good News about Jesus is integrated in practical ways into all areas of life. The challenge is to enlist people in carrying out strategies that have proven to encourage the growth of godly virtues in children of all ages.

One of the training sessions contains plans designed to help your staff, both newly recruited and experienced, to increase their effectiveness in building Christian character.

A Lot More Than Teaching

A few years ago I decided to purchase and learn to use a computer. As I began to investigate, there were so many choices! Did I want a word processor or a graphic program? I thought I knew what graphics were, but what was a word processor? Anything like my food processor? I didn't want my writing shredded! And there was software and hardware; "k's" and "bytes"; screens—monochrome and color!

Fortunately, a friend came along and said, "Vernie, you are trying to take on too much at once. Let me teach you how to use a simple program. Get a little training. Then you will discover the joy of working on a computer." Good thinking! And it worked. I thoroughly enjoy my computer, and I continue to learn better and more efficient ways to use it all the time.

The assignment of recruiting can be overwhelming, but take one step at a time. Let's look at how the variety of programs we call *children's ministry* is able to give support to a recruiting strategy.

Variety, the Spice of Recruitment

There is a wide variety of tasks available to those willing to serve in children's ministry. Not everyone wants to be a teacher, nor is teaching the only work to be done. Everyone needs to be successful as he begins to serve. Some may be ready to teach. Others may wish to be secretaries, photographers, musicians, or assistants. Loving, caring adults may serve in a classroom by providing help and encouragement for a child needing individual attention. Special projects may temporarily involve those who have special interests or skills. All of these roles provide the opportunity to observe teachers in action and to experience the joy of being with children. At the same time, the teacher's initial desire to serve and teach is kept alive rather than destroyed by inexperience and overload. One other benefit of this kind of programming is that teachers are more easily recruited when they have support people. Teamwork becomes a reality.

Short Term or Long Term?

A long-term commitment is usually a school or calendar year, or more. This kind of commitment, while difficult to achieve among all staff volunteers, is the *best* option for the children. Working toward a long-term commitment with your staff allows greater opportunity for the adults to build meaningful relationships and disciple children. Effective, life-changing teaching takes place over a longer period of time. Sunday school as well as afternoon or weeknight club or youth group programs allow for this kind of spiritual nurturing.

Offer several levels of staff commitment in your children's programming. Some people would never consider serving as a Sunday school teacher for a year, but they may find a week of Vacation Bible School a rewarding way to be involved. Public- and private-school teachers frequently enjoy a shorter term of involvement. There is the opportunity to be a counselor at day camp or overnight camps. Many children's ministries are providing field trips, one-day-a-week experiences for children, throughout the summer. There is the person who volunteers for nursery duty one Sunday a month. Others may volunteer for childcare one day a week to allow mothers of preschoolers to have a "Mother's Day Out." And, of course, there is the wonderful role of substitute. Individuals become part of the substitute list and agree to remain on the list for a specific length of time. These short-term commitments can become the training ground for a longer-term teaching role.

Total Programming

A view of programming to meet the many needs of children through several opportunities, not just in one hour, creates a relaxed feeling among all staff. The staff you recruit can be assured that no one person is expected to accomplish everything. The children's choir enhances the Sunday school music program. The club or youth-group program helps to build relationships as well as reinforce Sunday school experiences. Special events may provide enriching activities as well as opportunities to respond to Bible truths. The larger the variety of roles in which to serve, the larger the number of people who will find a place to use their gifts.

Program to Meet Today's Needs

Consider programming to meet special needs; adults as well as children will benefit. Hotlines for kids, support groups for single parents, after-school clubs for children with both parents working, and classes in English as a second language are only a few of the possibilities you may wish to consider. Be aware of the special needs in your area. Staff who serve in these ministries might never respond to teaching a Sunday school class or leading a youth group.

Maintain and expand programs that meet needs. Stop programs that no longer are effective.

Sharing the Responsibility

In "days of old," firefighters counted on a "fire brigade" to help fight fires, a line of people extending from the fire to the source of water. Buckets of water were filled and passed from hand to hand until they reached the person at the end of the line, who poured the water on the fire. The many hands of the brigade made it possible to extinguish the fire.

Chapter Two

Take a good look at the tasks you and your staff are doing. How can you be handing "buckets of water" to one another? Are there ways to lighten the preparation load? How can you release your staff to have more time for prayer, for lesson preparation, for building relationships and discipling the children in their classes?

Here are two examples of creative programs that have produced support for teachers and provided new workers with exposure to children's ministry and the development of spiritual gifts.

A small group of women called the "Friday Ladies" gather at a church in Southern California every Friday. Their task is to do all the busy work that is such an important part of children's ministry. They cut, paste, collate, and staple. They make signs, name tags, felt boards, and bulletin boards.

The "Friday Ladies" meeting has become a place of fellowship and prayer that enables many, in time, to teach children themselves. Many people who would initially tremble at the prospect of facing a classroom filled with live children are more than willing to help out with tasks they view as safer. Over time, their interest grows in the outcome of the work they have contributed. And the next time they are asked to consider stepping into a direct ministry role, the reluctance is greatly diminished.

"Caring Hands" is a program of partnership between parents and the church. Parents who are regular attenders of the church are asked to give one month of service for each child in their family. Volunteers receive a letter and a packet of materials with specific details about their one-month task. These parents become support people in the classrooms, not teachers. In the process they observe, learn, and practice with experienced teachers.

Parents who participate become excited about knowing what their children are learning. Some discover for the first time the importance of a committed teacher in the lives of their children. Support from parents increases. Some become full-time teachers; all have a greater understanding of the importance of teaching children. Teachers have help in their classrooms, and relationships with parents are built. Nobody loses in a program such as this.

List some tasks that you or your teachers do that could be done by others. How could your church creatively program to get these jobs done and involve others in the joy of ministry to children?

_____

_____

_____

_____

_____

_____

Chapter Three

Recruitment Challenges

One of the most exciting events at a track meet is the hurdles. The runners must combine speed with precise timing to clear each hurdle smoothly, regain their stride, and clear the next barrier, and the next. To win the race, every hurdler knows what must be done. The goal is clearly defined, and the runners know what it takes to reach it.

Hurdling is an exacting skill, much of the training is concerned with technique—approach, stride pattern, hurdle clearance. All technique practice must be done at speed. Training goes on each day, every day, no matter how tired an athlete might be or how boring the routine may become.

There is a parallel here for all recruiters. *Our success depends greatly on knowing the obstacles ahead, plus the strategy, the practice, and the pacing that must be maintained to succeed.*

As a hurdler begins to prepare for a race, you would not hear any complaints about the ten hurdles that lie ahead; they are part of the race. The runner expects to know weariness and disappointment as well as the exhilaration of winning.

Roger Kingdom, two-time Olympic gold-medal winner said, "When I get out on the track, . . . I have to give it my best, win or lose. I can't say, 'I had a bad day,' or 'I was out too late last night.' I have to feel very, very good about the race. . . . I have to give it everything I have. That's what people like to see. They like to see someone who doesn't quit."

As recruiters we face a race filled with obstacles and hurdles. It is important that we clearly identify them and build a strategy for overcoming them. Perseverance is a vital character trait needed by each recruiter. Never, never give up! *Recruitment must become a continuous process.*

It is not possible to stand at the starting line and say, "Remove hurdles one, five, and seven, and then I'll run the race." Haven't you heard these "If only you would remove the hurdle" phrases?

"Our church is so small, there aren't enough people to work with children."

"Our church is so large and there are so many tasks to accomplish, there are never enough people for children's ministry."

"We have lost our volunteer force. All the women are working away from home now."

"We have too many single parents and blended families. These people face so much stress, they couldn't possibly get involved in teaching."

"We just can't compete with soccer and Little League and all the other recreation programs for kids and parents."

These statements may be accurate, to a point. But we need to capture the vision that we can do an effective job of recruiting as we gain skills and use strategies to clear the hurdles. And as with an athlete running for the gold, we must stay in training, run the course, and get ready for the next event.

Paul's use of the racing metaphor in Hebrews 12:1-4 may have great significance to those of us called to this ministry. Perhaps the verses could be viewed as the recruiter's "gold."

> "Therefore, since we are surrounded by such a great cloud of witnesses, let us throw off everything that hinders and the sin that so easily entangles, and let us run with perseverance the race marked out for us. Let us fix our eyes on Jesus, the author and perfector of our faith, who for the joy set before him endured the cross, scorning its shame, and sat down at the right hand of the throne of God. Consider him who endured such opposition from sinful men, so that you will not grow weary and lose heart. In your struggle against sin, you have not yet resisted to the point of shedding your blood" (*NIV*).

Probably one-third of the children's ministry director's time needs to be spent on recruiting. Recruiting is everybody's job, but the children's director is the most likely person to recruit, train, motivate, and develop volunteers. Let's begin by identifying the hurdles. It will be helpful for us as recruiters to remember that these obstacles have two sides—the recruiter's perspective and that of the recruit. Often these two perspectives are very different. Both affect the planning of our strategy.

Communication

How do you communicate the need for well-staffed children's ministry? A beginning place may be an attitude check. Do you hold the perspective that serving in children's ministry is one of the most rewarding opportunities for members of your congregation? When you recruit, be sure you are presenting opportunities for service rather than a desperate need to fill vacancies.

Positive communication includes attractive areas that display and define roles in which people can choose to serve. Pictures of classrooms, children, teachers, and events give a visual message. Invite a few adults at a time to visit a class in action. Report positive facts about children and their children's staff in your church newsletter on a regular basis. Create intentional strategies for proclaiming to your congregation that reaching children is a number-one priority, not the second-best place or the fourth or fifth or last place to serve.

Serving is a kingdom principle, in spite of what our culture may say about putting self first. The King himself declared that he "did not come to be served, but to serve" (Matthew 20:28). Everyone who follows the leadership of that servant king is setting out upon a quest of service. And serving in children's ministry is enabling young people to serve Jesus for all the days of their lives. This leads us to our next hurdle, commitment.

Commitment

Commitment to others has not been a big part of our culture in recent decades. The catch phrases of society have gone from "Do your own thing!" to "The Me Generation" to "Look Out for #1!" Commitment to self has been viewed as more desirable than commitment to others or to God. Recruiters in churches are often highly discouraged as people rehearsed their need to be gone on weekends and involved in many activities away from church. This emphasis to be elsewhere may not be all bad, but like many other choices, in excess it becomes destructive. As people become unavailable, more selective in their use of time, often the time is not used to serve others.

Many organizations outside the church have sought to cope with the challenge of a self-centered culture. National leaders have issued calls for people to step forward and offer to help where needs exist. These calls for volunteers have become both a blessing and an obstacle. As people are being motivated to volunteer, many highly visible, professional, or appealing groups also are actively recruiting them. How do we compete with the challenge in a video produced by a high-powered ad agency? How do we respond when the people we approach have already committed themselves to coaching soccer? Still, the attitudes being fostered by many agencies in our society do help create a fertile field for recruiting volunteers for children's ministry.

One other hurdle we need to label as we consider commitment is the commitment of the recruiter. That means dedication to setting goals, establishing job descriptions, creating intentional and ongoing training, developing leadership to recruit, caring for the "troops," and regularly evaluating the effectiveness of our recruitment strategies. Sometimes it is too easy to blame the unwillingness of others to get involved when at least some of the problem is our own lack of effective planning and consistent follow-through. Chapters 4-10 present a very workable recruiting plan that can help any recruiter who makes the commitment to do this great work as effectively as possible.

Attitude

Our attitudes can affect our commitment. We all have "attitude attacks," moments when we feel discouraged or defeated. Make a responsible plan to overcome these common recruiter attitudes:

"I'll never have all the workers I need."

"It all depends on me."

"There will never be enough people."

"Our church is too small (or too big)."

"I love working with children, but I hate recruiting others to work with children."

"Children's workers are baby-sitters."

"I always feel like I'm begging people."

"It's usually easier to do things myself than try to get someone else to help."

Create a mind-set for yourself, as an athlete does. Let's go back to our illustration of the hurdler. Roger Kingdom said, "I can say I ran a bad race because I stayed out too late, but the truth is, I chose not put the race first."

What is your choice concerning the children's ministry of your congregation? How do you impart an excitement and reward for recruiting? Is it your perspective that the glass is half empty or half full? Do you see only how many more there are to recruit (slots to be filled), or are you and those who recruit with you able to rejoice in the one recruited (winning the race) and to be excited about the next person who will respond?

In our culture, a difficult job is a job to be avoided. Many pastors and Christian educators say to children's directors, "Oh, you have the hardest job in the church." What they communicate is "You have the worst job in the church."

The athlete will never be a track star if he sees the difficult job of training and practicing as undesirable. Exercise the character trait of responsibility by setting goals, attaining goals, and overcoming obstacles. Become increasingly dependent upon God to accomplish the recruitment task, which is not to fill all the vacant positions on our organization chart. The recruitment task is to engage people in the excitement of ministry, ministry that accomplishes these powerful goals in the lives of children.

- Win them to Christ.
- Teach them to know and apply God's Word.
- Build positive relationships and develop their conscience and character toward God.
- Equip them to serve.

Competence

This hurdle, especially, has two sides, that of the recruiter and that of the recruit. The recruiter may feel incompetent. Have these thoughts or statements ever been yours?

"I can't recruit people."

"I don't have the skills to develop a teaching staff."

"I can't talk people into doing things."

"How do you equip and train people?"

And at the same time a prospective recruit is saying,

"I don't know how to teach or work with children."

"I've never taught a child."

"I don't know how to do crafts or music."

Overcoming the competence obstacle requires training and practice. Recruiters, identify others who know how to recruit and ask them to coach you. Attend every workshop and read every book about recruitment you can find. (Congratulations, you have already begun! You are reading this book.) If you need help setting up training, use the training sessions at the back of this book. Check the list of suggested training resources on page 63 as well.

It is largely up to you to help those you recruit both feel able and learn to truly be competent. Guarantee training opportunities. Set up times for observing in classes. Create a support system using experienced volunteers.

Burnout

Burnout is a word we would all like to avoid! Recruiters often hear "burnout" as the reason for a decision to stop teaching or for not accepting a teaching ministry. There are several practical steps that can be taken to prevent and overcome burnout.

• *Lack of staff* sometimes perpetuates itself by causing existing staff to be overworked and frustrated in their service. When the adult/child ratio is out of balance, great frustration is the result. Nursery rooms need one adult for every two or three children.

Recruitment Challenges

Twos and threes need one adult for every two or three children. Fours and fives need one adult for every four or five children. In the elementary grades, one adult is needed for every six to eight children. These ratios take into consideration that attendance patterns of children, especially the youngest ones, can fluctuate significantly. Even on those Sundays when almost every child happens to show up, a staff organized by proper ratios can make sure that each child gets the personal attention needed. However, if staffing is based on the lowest attendance, workers can expect numerous weeks when they are harried and hurried and children's needs are overlooked.

When consistent effort is being made to recruit enough staff, both new recruits and those who are already involved will find increased joy and fulfillment in working with children. Quality teaching and strong relationships become an expected part of the ministry. Lives of children are changed. The time spent together becomes calm and pleasant.

• *Inadequate space* may cause frustration and disappointment in ministry to children. Assist teachers as they strive to work in rooms that may not be ideal. Offer creative ideas for room arrangement. Be sure that careful attention is given to cleanliness and maintenance of the facilities.

• *Fuzzy communication* may be a factor in burnout. Working in a ministry without clear direction leads to a feeling of uneasiness. Both verbal and written communication is essential. Leaders need to be available for questions and encouraging words. Guidelines, expectations, and announcements that focus on the goals of your ministry anticipate the need for information and provide it before frustration occurs.

• *Encouragement* and *affirmation* are two elements that will help prevent burnout. People do not become involved in children's ministry in order to receive encouragement and affirmation, but their response when they get it is always positive! Continued ministry with children is often the result of interaction with staff in this way.

• *A strong, ongoing recruitment program* encourages staff to stay involved with children. Recruitment for a specified length of time removes the concern that anyone will be expected to "teach forever." Prospective staff members will become aware of ongoing concern and efforts to support them if they choose to serve in ministry to children.

• *Change in the lives of staff members* may require a change in ministry. Recognize changes. Sometimes as we change, we desire a change in ministry. Remove the feeling of guilt when an individual asks to leave children's ministry to begin serving in another area. Encourage each one to recognize and develop gifts from God and to seek his guidance. Expecting and accepting change is an important factor in reducing burnout.

Approach burnout with a positive attitude. Believe that much of it can be prevented, and then use your initiative to activate a plan that is uniquely designed for your church.

Over the years, numerous polls looking at the religious consciousness of America have shown that as many as ninety percent of American parents want their children to have religious education. How are our churches responding to this desire? Recruiting and developing staff for the programs to meet the changing needs of children and their families is a great challenge. We have to learn to clear the hurdles!

Compassion for the changes in people's lives, forgiveness and flexibility in meeting people's needs, and integrity and variety in plans and programs are essential steps in getting over barriers. Continuous prayer and a plan for continued recruitment will enable recruiters to identify and motivate staff. You will discover a double reward as you assist adults to become involved in ministry and see children being reached for God.

An Invitation to Ministry

The process that will be described in this chapter and the next has proven effective in many children's ministries. The foundation of the process is the recruiter's belief that teaching children is one of the most important ministries in which one can choose to serve Christ. The process also assumes the perspective that God is the one who calls people to teach.

Perhaps many in your church are unaware that God expects them to serve. Dr. Wesley R. Willis described five levels of readiness for service in an article called "Stop Singing the Recruiting Blues." Level one is the "unaware/aware" level.

According to Dr. Willis, everyone in the average congregation can be assigned to one of two categories, unaware or aware. That is, unaware of God's expectations, or aware that God wants all to serve. A congregation of unaware people rarely will be responsive to challenges to serve, but all Christians can progress as they become aware of what God expects. Ordinarily it is best when the minister communicates from the pulpit what God expects; Christian education begins with the preaching of God's Word. Biblical instruction will help Christians to become aware that God expects them to serve.

The role of the recruiter is to present the challenge to serve in the most positive manner possible.

Identifying Potential Workers

Before you challenge someone to serve, first identify those who are most apt to respond positively. Look around you. Where will you find these people?

• Begin by keeping your eyes and your ears wide open. Observe the people in your congregation. Discover the people who interact positively with children. Who takes time to talk with them in the halls or after the service?

• Which members of your church are beginning to participate in church activities outside of Sunday-morning worship? Often these people are growing spiritually and may be looking for a place to serve.

• Are there young people in junior and senior high (both boys and girls) who are serious-minded and can take direction well? They need to be with their own classes most of the time, but they can make wonderful helpers on a once-a-month or once-a-quarter basis. If you have a two-hour program on Sunday morning, schedule young people so that they alternate missing Sunday school and missing the worship service.

• Are there college students majoring in education in your congregation? They may appreciate the opportunity to serve as enrichment for their college work.

• Some churches successfully use parents in their children's ministry programs. While parents should never be required to serve, helping in a classroom or other group program can help develop parenting skills. Be sure to include both mothers and fathers in this way.

• Senior citizens, both men and women, are often overlooked. Many have a wonderful capacity to befriend children who need one-on-one attention.

• Some adult Sunday school classes may be willing to adopt a specific children's class as a "home missions" project for one year, providing staff, materials, or whatever kinds of support are needed.

A Very Special Meeting

After you have identified a number of potential children's staff, invite them to attend a very special, forty-five-minute meeting. Clearly describe that the goal of the meeting is to acquaint people with children's ministry and the opportunities to serve in this vital program.

You may issue your invitations over the phone, in the church bulletin or newsletter, or in person. A personal contact is often more effective than the bulletin or newsletter. However, the use of *all* forms of advertising will keep your ministry visible.

Your conversation with a prospect might sound something like this:

"Good morning, Steven! I am calling (made a point to find you this morning) to invite you to a special gathering. It's for parents and others whom our staff has identified as having the kind of relationship with God that we desire for those serving in our children's ministry.

"This will be a forty-five-minute meeting at (time, place, date.) You will gain a better understanding of the exciting things happening through this ministry in our church. You will have an opportunity to ask questions, make comments, and consider what it means to serve Christ in a ministry to children. Would you be able to come?"

If the answer is yes, respond something like this: "I look forward to seeing you there. I'll drop a reminder to you in the mail three days before our meeting."

You are always recruiting, so if someone says, "No, that isn't a good time," find out when would be a good time. Create a prospect file, listing the times that prospects choose. When you have two or more prospects willing to come at a common time, schedule a meeting.

Building Respect

Time is valuable. By keeping your invitation short and concise and setting a time limit for the meeting, you communicate to your prospects that you value their time. This helps them begin to trust your ability to meet your staff's needs and give respect and support.

Always have at least several prospects at a meeting. People interact with each other; they discover that they have similar needs, concerns, and fears. This also helps

An Invitation to Ministry

you begin to build trust that this is a ministry in which people are not left to flounder on their own.

Advertise your ministry to the congregation. Use the church newsletter and bulletin to let people know what is happening. When prospects perceive that there is order and planning and enthusiasm within the children's ministry program, they are more inclined to want to be involved.

A Continuous Process

Always be watching for prospects and working to generate potential recruits. Here are some ideas to help you:
- Be sure you receive a new-members' list each time one is published.
- Create a prospect file.
- Adapt the "Christian Service Questionnaire" at the end of this chapter to survey your church membership. It is usually wise to avoid putting too many specific tasks on a questionnaire. By the time you tabulate long lists of responses, the questionnaire could be out of date. Instead, suggest general areas in which people can get involved and offer to follow up with more detailed information on current ministry opportunities. And make sure that everyone who completes a survey receives a prompt response. If there are too many people to quickly contact personally, invite them to an information meeting. Don't let anyone be justified in complaining that "I volunteered, but nobody ever talked to me about it."
- Create a list of public- and private-school teachers. They make wonderful summer and Vacation Bible School workers.
- Hold an open house for parents and grandparents, having them sign in as they enter. Each one present has demonstrated an interest in children, and becomes an excellent prospect.

CHRISTIAN SERVICE QUESTIONNAIRE

Name _____ Today's date _____

Address _____

_____

Phone _____ E-mail _____

Age ❏ 0–17 ❏ 18–30 ❏ 30–40 ❏ 40–50 ❏ 50–60 ❏ 60+ Status ❏ Married ❏ Single ❏ Widowed

Names/ages of children _____

_____

Current employment _____ Work phone _____

What leadership or teacher training have you had? Please describe.

Present service in the church:

Are you available during the day? ❏ Yes ❏ No

Are you currently in an adult small group? ❏ Yes ❏ No

What are your spiritual gifts? (See Romans 12; 1 Corinthians 12; Ephesians 4.)

Check all the spaces that apply.

	Have done	Desire to prepare		Have done	Desire to prepare		Have done	Desire to prepare
CHURCH LEADERSHIP			Secretary	❏	❏	Publicity	❏	❏
Elder	❏	❏	Pianist	❏	❏	Artwork	❏	❏
Deacon/deaconess	❏	❏	Preparation of materials	❏	❏	Drama	❏	❏
Committee member	❏	❏	Children's worship	❏	❏	Sew costumes	❏	❏
CHRISTIAN EDUCATION			Nursery	❏	❏	Bus driver (class 2)	❏	❏
Committee member	❏	❏	Vacation Bible School	❏	❏	**MUSIC**		
Leadership training	❏	❏	Library/resource center	❏	❏	Children's choirs:	❏	❏
Sunday school:			Athletic programs	❏	❏	Director	❏	❏
Division director	❏	❏	**SPECIAL EDUCATION**			Pianist	❏	❏
Coordinator	❏	❏	Signing for the deaf	❏	❏	Choir parent	❏	❏
Department leader	❏	❏	Teach special ed. class	❏	❏	Sing in choir	❏	❏
Teacher			**OUTREACH**			Solo work	❏	❏
Early childhood	❏	❏	Outreach leader	❏	❏	Instrumentalist	❏	❏
Children	❏	❏	Caller	❏	❏	Orchestra	❏	❏
Junior high	❏	❏	Prayer group	❏	❏	Song leader	❏	❏
Senior high	❏	❏	**SERVICES**			**CHURCH OFFICE**		
College	❏	❏	Usher	❏	❏	Typing	❏	❏
Career	❏	❏	Greeter	❏	❏	Newsletter	❏	❏
Adults	❏	❏	Audiovisual	❏	❏	Computer	❏	❏

An Invitation to Serve

Most of this chapter is written as a script for you to use in directing the information meeting to which you have invited your prospects. (See Chapter 4.) It is important to enable those who attend to learn quite a bit about ministry to children. Your goal for this meeting is to make it possible for recruits to choose a place of service. Obviously, you won't want to read the script to your prospects, as it is important that your own personality and vision are presented. Use the suggested presentation as a resource to prepare your own remarks. The suggested activities have been used in many such meetings and have been effective in helping people to thoughtfully consider the ministry that fits them best.

You will need photocopies of several handouts for all participants. Sample forms are provided at the end of this chapter. The forms are "Concerns and Rewards," "Time Requirements," "What Do You Normally Do in a Week?" and three job descriptions. The "Time Requirements" and job descriptions will need to be adapted to fit the needs of your own ministry. For example, you may want to develop several "Time Requirements" sheets, each for different children's ministries (Sunday school, children's church, weekday clubs, etc.). You may want to prepare sheets for some tasks that require less time commitment than the samples shown. However, people are more likely to be drawn towards the "easier" tasks, leaving you the challenge of trying to encourage some people to consider the more demanding tasks instead.

"Thank you for attending this meeting. You were promised that we would be here for forty-five minutes, and we plan to honor that commitment. We will be exploring some information about one of the most important and vital ministries of our church—ministry to our children. This is an opportunity for you to gather information, make comments, and ask questions. **You will not be asked to become a part of this ministry today**. Instead, it is our prayer that this time together will enable you to prayerfully consider ministry to children as part of your service to our Lord.

"Please take a photocopy of the 'Concerns and Rewards' sheet. *Distribute this handout.* Imagine with me that you have agreed to teach fourth-grade children. As you think about the task, what concerns, fears, and needs come to your mind? List your concerns and fears as quickly as possible under 'Concerns.'"

Allow three minutes for this task. Ask participants to share their concerns. List their responses on a transparency or chalkboard. The list will probably include:
"What are fourth graders like?"
"Will I be able to control them?"
"How do I keep their attention?"
"What material will be provided?"

"How do I get help?"
"Do I have enough time for this?"

"By listing our concerns, you can see that all of us here have many similar ones.

"If I could guarantee that all the concerns and needs listed will be cared for, how would you feel about serving in children's ministry? *Allow time for responses.*

"We *can* guarantee that all of these concerns and fears will be cared for, except for one, and that is *time.* Time management is a challenge for all of us. However, time invested in the lives of children has the potential of making a significant contribution to our church, our community, our country, and to God's kingdom. Let's look at a chart that will provide some guidelines for the time required for a variety of positions within our children's ministry.

Distribute the "Time Requirements" chart. Adapt your comments to fit the tasks in your church's ministries.

"If you choose to serve as a teacher in this ministry, your commitment is to prepare two hours for each week's session, to arrive in the classroom fifteen minutes before class, to spend thirty minutes each week contacting your students by card or phone, and to attend a two-hour monthly training/planning meeting. You also are asked to have one social event for your class per teaching term to help build positive relationships within the group and to encourage Christian character development.

"Time invested in preparation and training is essential. Serving in this ministry requires a high level of commitment. Our standards are high, not because we want to add a lot of work to your life, but because we have discovered what it takes in order to succeed in this ministry. We are not asking you to clutter up your life with busy work. We are inviting you to serve with us in making a life-changing impact on children. We are sharing with young people who are important to God now. They will become tomorrow's leaders. They will help shape the future.

"We have prepared a worksheet that you may want to use to help you determine the amount of time you can invest in serving. *Distribute the "What Do You Normally Do in a Week?" sheet.* Take this home with you. Each day, write in the activities that are a regular part of your life and the number of hours you spend on each. You may find that you do indeed have available time that could be invested in children's ministry. Or you may find that your time is already filled with other activities. If that is the case, you may want to evaluate the proportion of your time that is given in service to the Lord. You may want to make adjustments in other areas to free up time you can use in service.

"On average, you will need three hours a week plus two hours per month for training and planning to be a coordinator or superintendent. Teachers need about four hours per week for preparation, teaching, and student contact, plus two hours per month for training and planning. If you have ever been part of a choir ministry, you know that you commit one to two hours on Sunday and one to two hours for practice during the week. This same kind of time commitment holds true if you are teaching adults or youth. So if you are already serving in these areas, you would not want to serve in our children's ministry unless you have a great deal of time available.

"While you are considering the time you have available to serve, ask God, 'Are you calling me to serve these boys and girls?' We want to inform and challenge you to serve with us reaching children for Christ. To that end, we want you to ask God about

An Invitation to Serve

this opportunity and then let us know what he is telling you."

Conclude your informational meeting by discussing the procedure for making a commitment to children's ministry.

"If you choose to become a part of this ministry, we are committed to equipping, training, and supporting you. To accomplish this, we will have a two-hour training/planning meeting once a month. The items you have listed as your concerns become our training topics. Our guarantee to help conquer your concerns and fears is directly related to your attendance at these meetings."

Take a few moments at this point to introduce any other leaders who work with you in providing this support to staff members.

"Our commitment to you includes providing attractive and adequate classrooms and curriculum and supplies appropriate for the age level you choose to serve. You also will be given the names, addresses, phone numbers, and parent information needed to maintain your contact commitment. In addition, you will be linked up with at least one other ministry partner, as we are committed to ministry in teams. Just as Jesus sent his disciples out in pairs, our children's ministry is built on serving together, encouraging and supporting one another. We also structure our ministry by teams to ensure safety for our children.

Pass out the "Guidelines for Children's Safety" handout and briefly mention the importance of these guidelines in your ministry.

"What questions or comments do you have?" *Allow time for responses.*

"Now it is time for us to look at the other half of the 'Concerns and Rewards' sheet. If you become a part of this ministry with children, what do you think the rewards will be? What kind of rewards would motivate you to become a part of this team? Take a few minutes to jot down your ideas."

Once again, ask participants to share their ideas. List them on an overhead transparency or chalkboard. The list probably will include:
"I would enjoy learning more about the Bible."
"I would be happy to influence a child for life."
"I would know how to teach my own children about God."
"I enjoy the enthusiasm of children."

After making a list, ask, "Are you interested? Would you like to be a part of changing these young lives? We have tried to provide you with a view of our value of children and the need and opportunity to serve Christ in ministry to children. Now it is time for you to ask God, 'Do you want me to serve you by working with the children of this church?'

"Please write your name, address, and phone number on your 'Concerns and Rewards' sheet and give it to me before you go.

"Take your 'What Do You Normally Do in a Week?' sheets home and begin to evaluate your use of time. Talk to God and ask for his direction. Our children need (number) staff to serve with us from (month) to (month).

Chapter Five

"Each of these positions has a job description that is available tonight. You may take any of the job descriptions with you to help you with the decision-making process.

"You will receive a phone call from me in five to seven days. You can let me know what God is asking you to do in relation to the children in our church. If you wish to call me before then, please do. If there is any further information you need, I'll be here for at least fifteen minutes after I close, or you may call me anytime this week.

End the meeting with prayer, asking God to guide your children's ministry and help the meeting attenders in their decision-making process.

Following Up

The "Concerns and Rewards" sheets become your follow-up sheets. Keep your commitment to call each person within five to seven days. Some of them may call you.

Respond to "I don't have enough time to teach" with an invitation to choose the task with the least time commitment—secretary (one and a half hours on Sunday morning and two hours training/planning monthly). Or you might ask, "Since now is not a good time, would you consider Vacation Bible School for one week this summer? Or afternoon club once a month? Or have you thought of teaching one month this summer? We try to give our regular workers some time off during the summer."

You can also respond to "no" answers with, "May I check back with you in six months to see if there is any change in God's call on your life?" File the names of these prospects in your prospect file.

Graciously accept refusals. Do not talk prospects into serving. Instead, encourage them to consider serving in another ministry that interests them.

Choosing to Serve

When a prospect says, "Yes, I believe God is asking me to serve in children's ministry," make a twenty-minute appointment to discuss his or her job description. Together fill out a "Staff Interview Sheet," another important step in commitment to children's ministry. A sample of this form is at the end of this chapter. Adapt it as necessary to meet your situation.

Most churches require that children's ministry staff be approved by a committee or board before they begin to serve. Make certain that all prospects understand at this time that their service will begin after that approval has been given.

You will notice that the "Staff Interview Sheet" contains a place for the prospect to list references. You may feel this is unnecessary in the church. Unfortunately, it is not. Authorities who deal with child abuse know that abusers often seek positions working with children in community-group settings. Some police departments have even recommended that churches run checks for prior arrests on all potential staff. Although asking for references and checking them are not completely adequate safeguards, they are steps in the right direction. It is important that you convey the attitude that your congregation is aware of the menace of child abuse and is prepared to confront it.

An
Invitation
to
Serve

TIME REQUIREMENTS

	COORDINATOR	SUPERINTENDENT	TEACHER	SECRETARY
WEEKLY	support and recruiting 🕐 1 hour Sunday morning 🕐 1 1/2 hours room environment, curriculum, and supplies 🕐 1/2 hour	preparation 🕐 1 hour Sunday morning 🕐 1 1/2 hours teacher contact 🕐 1/2 hour	preparation 🕐 2 hours Sunday morning 🕐 1 1/2 hours student contact 🕐 1/2 hour	Sunday morning 🕐 1 1/2 hours
MONTHLY	CE board meeting 🕐 2 hours training/planning meeting for all department workers 🕐 2 hours	preparation for training/planning meeting 🕐 2 hours meeting 🕐 2 hours	training/planing meeting 🕐 2 hours	training/planing meeting 🕐 2 hours

WHAT DO YOU NORMALLY DO IN A WEEK?

For one week, record activities that are a regular part of your life.
Indicate the number of hours that you spend in each activity.

SUNDAY	MONDAY	TUESDAY	WEDNESDAY	THURSDAY	FRIDAY	SATURDAY

Do you have time available for ministry? Is all of your time already committed? Evaluate the amount of time you spend serving the Lord in ministry. Are there areas where you can make adjustments?

CHILDREN'S MINISTRY JOB DESCRIPTION

AGE-LEVEL COORDINATOR

(volunteer position)

The coordinator ministers under the supervision of the elder responsible for children's ministry and/or the director of children's ministry.

FUNCTION

To provide leadership and encouragement and to oversee the comprehensive program in Christian education for an assigned age group(s) or grade(s).

To develop a personal ministry to the volunteer department leaders of the designated age group(s) or grade(s), no fewer than three people nor more than six.

RESPONSIBILITIES

1. Be accountable to the elder responsible for children's ministry and/or the director of children's ministry.
2. Attend a monthly Christian education board meeting for spiritual leadership, skill development, and goal setting.
3. Organize and administer the Christian education program of the designated department. This includes prayer, room environment, supplies, philosophy, curriculum, staffing, outreach, follow-up, scheduling, and evaluation.
4. Meet monthly with the superintendent(s) of designated department(s).
5. Communicate status and needs of department(s).
6. Work closely with others involved with music, missions, recruiting, training, outreach, and evaluation.
7. Once per quarter, evaluate each superintendent with guidance and support of the responsible elder and/or director of children's ministry.
8. Faithfully attend and participate in the Sunday-morning worship service.

CHILDREN'S MINISTRY JOB DESCRIPTION

DEPARTMENT SUPERINTENDENT

(volunteer position)

The superintendent(s) will minister under the supervision of an age-level coordinator.

RESPONSIBILITIES

1. Meet once a month with age-level coordinator.
2. Meet once a month with teachers of the department to plan in detail the lessons for the following unit.
3. Coordinate the activities of the department.
4. Be a resource person for the teachers in the department.
5. Function as a channel of communication between the coordinator and the teachers.
6. Oversee the ministry of secretaries.
7. Assist in recruiting workers for your department.
8. Assist in setting up student class assignments for September.
9. Be responsible for materials needed for use by teachers.
10. Be responsible for the appearance of the room used by the department.
11. Be responsible for overseeing departmental contacts:
    - Collect contact sheets each week.
    - Update member and visitor cards.
    - Contact any teachers who have not made calls.
    - Assist teachers in contacting absentees when asked.
12. Plan to serve for twelve months.
13. Encourage, affirm, and support teachers who serve in the department.
14. Faithfully attend and participate in the Sunday-morning worship service.

CHILDREN'S MINISTRY JOB DESCRIPTION

TEACHER FOR TWOS THROUGH SIXTH GRADE

(volunteer position)

Teachers will minister under the supervision of the department superintendent.

RESPONSIBILITIES

1. Pray regularly for and show a genuine spiritual concern for each student.
2. Be faithful in attendance and punctual each week. Arrive in class fifteen minutes before starting time.
3. As needed, secure a substitute from the list provided and notify the department superintendent.
4. Be faithful in contacting students:
    - Update enrollment list and visitor list weekly.
    - Phone, visit, or correspond with each absentee weekly and with regular attenders periodically.
    - Fill out a student contact sheet weekly.
    - Return contact sheet to the department secretary each week, with or without recorded contacts.
    - Pick up new contact sheet each week.
6. Be interested in each student as a person, and plan at least one social activity for the class. Send birthday cards.
7. Attend and participate in training/planning meetings with the coordinator and department superintendent for Bible study, teacher enrichment, and planning for the coming unit of lessons.
8. Plan to teach for one year (September to August) with time off for vacation.
9. Faithfully attend and participate in the Sunday-morning worship service.

GUIDELINES FOR CHILDREN'S SAFETY

All workers and volunteers in the children's programs are part of a ministry team guided by designated children's ministry leaders. Everyone involved in the children's programs must comply with these policies to ensure a safe and secure environment for the children and staff.

1. Each group of children shall have a minimum of two responsible workers, at least one being an adult, present at all times.
2. For children up through kindergarten age, at least one worker will be enlisted for every five children. With elementary aged children, at least one worker for every eight children will be provided.
3. One or more supervisors will circulate among rooms whenever children's activities are being held. Parents and other approved observers are welcome to visit children's programs at any time. Window blinds and doors are to be kept open whenever possible.
4. When taking children to the rest room, workers are to supervise children of the same gender. When not possible, the worker is to stay at the rest room door until the child is finished in the stall. Children are to have as much privacy as possible when using the rest room. Workers may enter to assist only when absolutely necessary.
5. Changing diapers is to be done in a room with at least one other worker present. No child shall be left unattended on a changing table at any time.
6. Emergency evacuation procedures are clearly posted in every children's room. Workers are to guide children as a group to the designated safe area outside the building.
7. Children through kindergarten age are to signed in and out by the same parent or other responsible adult. Parents are to be informed of this requirement when they first bring their children.

Child Safety Guidelines taken from *The 21st Century Sunday School* by Wes Haystead, © 1995 Wesley Haystead

 # STAFF INTERVIEW SHEET

Date _____ Phone (home) _____ (work) _____

Name _____

Address _____
                                            Street

‾‾
City   State   Zip
Occupation _____ Best time to reach by phone _____

How long attended this church? _____ Member? ❑ Yes ❑ No Presently attending what service? _____

What other church(es) have you regularly attended over the past three years? _____

Other involvement at this church or with Christian organizations? _____

_____

How did you come to know Christ as your Savior? _____

_____

Position interested in _____

Experience _____

Training _____

References (2) _____

_____

Have you read our church's policies on child and youth safety and protection against abuse? ❑ Yes ❑ No

What questions do you have about these policies? _____

Have you ever been convicted or pleaded guilty to child abuse or a crime involving actual or attempted sexual molestation of a minor?
If yes, please explain. _____

Is there any other information we should know? _____

What are your greatest concerns as you contemplate this ministry? _____

_____

Have all of these areas been discussed with you today?
❑ Preparation   ❑ Curriculum   ❑ Weekly contacts   ❑ Visitation
❑ Training   ❑ Attendance records ❑ Socials   ❑ Arrival time

Comments: _____

_____

A Strategy for Caring

"When seeking to involve people in ministry, help the present staff to succeed. . . . A group of people who are accomplishing something worthwhile are powerfully effective in attracting others to get involved."[1]

When we meet the immediate felt needs of our staff, they tend to continue serving. When our staff continues serving, time and energy can be invested in recruiting and training people for future service rather than recruiting to fill immediate needs. Renewed staff commitments result in experienced staff, stronger staff/child relationships, and more effective learning and discipline of learners.

Doug, a children's pastor, asked Dave to arrive thirty minutes before Sunday school was scheduled to begin. For the past four years, Dave had faithfully taught active and challenging fourth-graders. As Dave knocked on Doug's door, it flew open, and Dave was greeted with cheers—a surprise party to express appreciation for his serving God through his fourth-grade class.

My experience has been that teachers who have been encouraged, commended, and well cared for have been happy to renew their commitments year after year.

Many of the staff we recruit do not initially consider themselves to be teachers. They catch the vision from the leader who recruits them and models Luke 6:40 for them: "A student is not better than his teacher. But when the student has fully learned all that he has been taught, then he will be like his teacher" (*ICB*). Intentionally plan strategies that will allow you to be compassionate, caring, and kind to existing staff as well as new recruits. Help them plan how to care for their support people and/or the children they serve. Consider these tested ideas.

Pray Together

Create a room where the staff can meet for prayer before class or after class. Providing for the staff's choice of time allows them to fit this important discipline into their schedules. Be sure to include designated times of prayer in your training/planning meetings also. Include personal prayer for the specific needs of staff as well as prayer for their learners.

Rejoice Together

Rejoice with staff when goals are achieved. To accomplish this, define the teaching role in terms of measurable goals, rather than just "success." It is one thing to "teach

IN APPRECIATION OF OUR TEACHERS

the third grade." It is quite another to evaluate the teaching/learning experience in relationship to measurable objectives. Guide teachers to set goals and objectives in addition to the lesson aims in your curriculum. Goals and objectives may be related to Bible content, relationships, the building of conscience and character, and observable response in applying God's Word. Consider goals and objectives like these:

• Children speak to each other in thoughtful, kind ways and are described as compassionate by their teachers and peers.

• Children work cooperatively to memorize Scripture passages. They are verbally recognized by staff and peers as choosing to cooperate in learning activities.

• Staff contacts each child individually with mail, phone calls, or a home visit to build the child's sense of worth and belonging.

• A class outing is planned to build community and relationships.

Provide a Back Up

Create a list of substitutes who may be called at any time during the week, even Saturday night or Sunday morning when a staff member's child wakes up ill. Recruit substitutes who are assigned to specific teachers. Challenge these substitutes to also become the prayer partners of "their" teachers.

Reward and Recognize

Build rewards and recognition into your ministry. Be sure all staff members, no matter their role, know they are loved and appreciated.

Choose to be an involved and evident leader. Periodic visits into the classroom tell staff that who they are and what they do is important enough for you to be in their class, supporting and demonstrating respect and care. Take time to be sure things are going well. If a teacher needs more masking tape, what better way to serve the teacher and learners than by allowing the teacher to remain with the class while the leader obtains the needed tape?

Use all the communication channels available to you to bring attention and praise to staff who are beginning a task or have successfully achieved a goal:

• *Place a large bouquet of flowers or a bunch of balloons in the church foyer* with a large sign: "In appreciation for our teachers."

• Enlist a person with an artistic flair to *design a bulletin board* that celebrates people on your teaching staff. Include photographs of teachers in action with children, hand-written notes of appreciation from students, and testimonials from teachers of why this ministry is important to them.

• *Present certificates of recognition.* You may think these will only be shoved in the back of a drawer, but this simple act of kindness and the effort to create a specific reward for your staff is a proven motivator.

• *Celebrate Thanksgiving Sunday* (the Sunday before Thanksgiving). Ask all parents to show appreciation to their children's teachers with verbal comments or written thank-you notes or small tokens of appreciation such as baked goods. Place a list of all those who serve in children's ministry in the church bulletin prior to this special Sunday.

A Strategy for Caring

• *Send birthday cards and anniversary cards* to all workers.

• *Plan a teacher-dedication service* at the beginning of each teaching term. This needs to take place during your worship service and be conducted by your minister(s).

• *Think of ways to move people from job to job* with appropriate lengths of "time off" in between. Secretaries observing teachers each Sunday may wish to try a summer term of teaching. Experienced teachers may become excellent department superintendents. Coordinators often wish to return to the classroom for a year of closer work with children.

• *Plan staff retreats.* Make times for family and friends of staff to meet each other. Play together, pray together, and be encouraged with special speakers or trainers.

• *Create a supply and preparation area or room.* Make it possible for staff to easily obtain, at the expense of your ministry, all the materials needed to accomplish the lesson plans outlined in the curriculum you have provided.

• *Maintain clean, well-lighted, well-equipped rooms.* This may involve everything from eliminating clutter, regularly updating bulletin boards, posters, or anything else displayed on the walls, to periodically repainting the walls, adding colorful trim, and replacing old, worn-out equipment. There are ways to accomplish this on a limited budget. Be careful you do not use "budget" as an excuse to settle for less than the very best for the students.

• *Plan personal follow-up and other special training* to encourage and show staff that you care for them and want them to be successful in their ministries. Target your coordinators and department superintendents. Invite them to your home. Attend one of their children's sporting or music events. Your personal interest in the lives of your leaders is the model for their personal involvement in the lives of the teachers and support staff they are serving and training.

• *Provide at least two other professional training times* for your staff each year. Fall and spring seem to be the times people need to hear an "outside" voice, saying what you always say but from a different perspective. If your budget doesn't allow you to invite a special speaker, create a trade with another local children's ministry leader: You teach one training session for her and she teaches one for you. Or perhaps one of the public- or private-school teachers in your church would be willing to do a training session on age-level characteristics or how children think and learn. Select a topic that would be a part of her professional experience but applicable to the Sunday school classroom as well.

Children's ministry cannot be accomplished without volunteers. "Having a ministry based on volunteers must also include having a ministry to volunteers. The strategy of recruitment, orientation, and training needs to be combined with the art of awareness, ongoing personal education, development, encouragement, and prayer."[2]

References

1 Haystead, Wes. *The 21st Century Sunday School: Strategies for Today and Tomorrow.* Cincinnati, OH: Standard Publishing, 1995, p. 144.

2 Haggerty, Philip E.; "Why Can't We Get Any Volunteers?" *Christian Education Today*, Fall 1989.

Preservice Training

Recruiting and training people for ministry is a process. A preservice training course is an important part of the process in which you guide people to discover their gifts and consider their responsibilities as members of the body of Christ. Also, you help them explore available ministry opportunities. Potentially everyone in the church is a candidate for this course.

The first step to beginning a training course is to think through several questions: when and where to meet, the length of the course, and who will be the instructor(s).

Offering the course at different times of the year may enable you to reach more people. When choosing a time in the week for the course to meet, your options might be:

- the Sunday-morning or Sunday-evening worship hour
- the Sunday school hour
- before or after any regularly scheduled service
- a midweek evening
- Friday night or Saturday morning or evening.

Reserve a room that is easily located and large enough to accommodate the number of people expected. (Twenty to thirty people is a good size for a class of this type.) Ideally you will need ten to fifteen square feet per person. The room needs to be clean, with good lighting and equipment; it is your "model" classroom.

The length of the class may vary. I have experienced greater participation with shorter sessions. Classes may meet weekly for fifty to sixty minutes for four to six weeks. People seem to be able to commit to four consecutive weeks. Assess the potential attendance patterns of your prospective staff.

One person can teach all four weeks of the course each time it is offered; however, it is not necessary that the responsibility remain solely with one person. You might consider having a different instructor for each topic. Or do some team teaching, especially with a topic such as ministry opportunities or age-level characteristics. The senior minister may want to be the instructor for the session concerning spiritual gifts. "Policies and Procedures Unique to Your Church" might be taught by the person responsible for overseeing Christian education.

The instructor needs to be a recognized leader in your congregation with educational skills and abilities. He needs to be personally involved with the educational ministries included in the course and have a commitment to them as well as to the congregation, its leadership, and the goals of the church. Instructors need to be friendly, spiritually mature, people of high moral character, and able to work well with people. Their goal for the class is to help those attending the course discover, develop, and use their spiritual gifts in the minstry of the church.

You can begin to see that this preservice training incorporates all church ministries, not only ministry to children. Remember that this course is only one part of a process.

Participants will become prime prospects because they have a foundation laid through identification of their spiritual gifts and choosing to serve from a Biblical perspective.

By now I hope you are saying, "This is great, but how do we choose topics?"

Let's review the goals. You want people to understand the kingdom principle that all believers are called to serve (2 Corinthians 9:12, 13; Ephesians 2:10; 4:11-15; Titus 2:14; 1 Peter 4:10). You also want people to discover that God has gifted each believer for making an important and unique contribution in the building up of the body (1 Corinthians 12:7; Ephesians 4:16; 1 Peter 4:10). Therefore, you will want to be sure to do at least one class on these two subjects. Perhaps you will choose to give both topics a session of its own. Check the resource list in this book for resources that can help you plan training on God's gifts for service.

Next, you want a broad overview of the opportunities to serve within your church. Involve a variety of leaders in this session. A presentation by a panel with a question-and-answer period would be helpful. A short slide or video program could be used to show "Ministry in Action." Plus, there is great value in having people observe a ministry group in action at another time during the week.

Last, you probably will want to inform people of policies and procedures that are unique to your church or minstry. These could include the mission statement or goals of your church, procedures for interviewing and approving teachers and other workers, working within the organizational structure, and communication flow.

A four-week course might look something like this:
- **Week 1** Discovering, Developing, and Using Your Spiritual Gifts
- **Week 2** Biblical Perspective of Serving
- **Week 3** Ministry Opportunities in our Church
- **Week 4** Policies and Procedures our Church has Adopted

Continue the preservice training as it is appropriate for specific areas of service in your church. Three basic sessions for those interested in continued exploration of children's ministry could be these:
- **Week 5** Age-Level Characteristics; Scheduling Sessions to Meet Children's Needs
- **Week 6** Using Curriculum to Plan and Prepare Lessons
- **Week 7** Classroom Management (Discipline)

Additional Suggestions

Keep attendance records. Decide how many sessions, if any, a person can miss to still be considered as having completed the course. Perhaps you will want to make it possible to make up absences in the next cycle. Placing value on attendance communicates the importance of the course.

The preservice course needs to be viewed as an integral part of the ongoing process and an integral part of the equipping and training of your church members. It is not a desperate attempt to recruit people!

The principles of the course and its strategy need to be shared and owned by all of those in leadership—the pastoral staff, Sunday school officers, elders, members of the Christian education committee, and leaders of other church ministries. Every ministry that receives recruits as a result of this course needs to be involved in the planning and preparation of preservice

Preservice Training

In-Service Training

We would all like to have every teacher we recruit be a graduate of preservice training. Reality and experience tell us, however, that we often need to have the recruited teacher begin teaching as soon as possible. In-service training is a strategy for placing the new teacher directly into the classroom, where training takes place through observation, assistant teaching, and team teaching.

The three parts of this strategy are 1) observing, 2) assisting with part of the teaching, and 3) team teaching in full partnership. What follows is a description of the tasks for the teacher-in-training and for the trainer. The trainer may be the children's director or division coordinator or a department superintendent.

If time and other circumstance permits, place the new teacher in the class where he or she will eventually serve. This provides opportunity for the person to begin building relationships with the learners and other staff, as well as begin to feel comfortable in the classroom. The new teacher will begin to learn classroom management techniques and routines appropriate to the specific group of children. A smooth transition occurs as this training strategy proceeds.

However, sometimes the teacher who is being replaced leaves before in-service training occurs, or the new teacher is being prepared to move into a class where major changes need to be made in the quality level of instruction. Be sure in-service training takes place anyway. Place the new teacher in the nearest age or grade level where there is at least one teacher who will provide a strong model of teaching skills, effective use of curriculum, and effective classroom-management techniques. Once the new teacher has learned from the experienced teacher, you can then move either teacher to the group that needs new leadership.

Observation

Before the teacher-in-training observes a class in action, arrange a thirty-minute planning time to prepare this person for what he or she will see. Begin the planning time with prayer. Use the age-appropriate "Lesson Planning Sheet" to go over lesson aims and the schedule for the hour. Also go over the "Observation Sheet" for the age group the teacher-in-training is observing. Samples of both of these forms are found at the end of this chapter. Encourage the teacher-in-training to make note of questions or comments throughout the observation time.

After the teacher-in-training observes a session, meet together again for fifteen to thirty minutes. This meeting is most effective if it takes place in the classroom directly after the observation, with one or all of the staff still present. Go over the "Observation Sheet" and allow the teacher-in-training to express concerns and fears and to ask questions about the approaches used. Invite the staff to share things they felt went well and things they felt could have been improved. Focus on those things that will provide the most effective training experience. Encourage the teacher-in-training to plan to assist with a brief portion of the lesson the following week as the observation period of training continues.

Continue to plan and evaluate with the teacher-in-training as you move through the sequence suggested on the "In-Service Training Chart" at the end of this chapter. Adapt the schedule to meet your specific needs.

Assist With Part of the Teaching

Teaching as an assistant is designed to give the teacher-in-training support while learning teaching skills and becoming acquainted with the children, the class schedule, curriculum, and resources.

Allow the teacher-in-training to choose to help with the parts of the session that seem easiest for her. That may be telling part of the Bible story, helping to guide a learning activity, or sharing the application of the story. The "In-Service Training Chart" gives some suggestions. Which part of the session the teacher-in-training chooses first doesn't matter. What is important is to help the new teacher feel confident and have a good experience the first time she begins to teach. In the weeks that follow, have the teacher-in-training help to lead a different or additional part of the session. It will not take long for the new teacher to feel comfortable guiding any part of the session.

Team Teaching

This part of the in-service strategy allows an ongoing time of training with an experienced teacher, perhaps as long as two curriculum units (usually eight weeks). For a time the trainer may serve as the team teacher, or an outgoing teacher may be teamed with the teacher-in-training.

Both teachers plan together, pray together, and work together. They share responsibility for every part of the session. This partnership approach prevents "team" teaching from becoming "turn" teaching, where each teacher takes a turn while the other takes a Sunday off. "Turn" teaching fractures the building of relationships with children and defeats the purpose of training the new teacher. Should either the trainer or the experienced teacher need a week off, the trainer needs to provide an experienced teacher as a substitute.

During the initial training weeks, the trainer or experienced teacher is to guide the teacher-in-training through the parts of the hour, allowing the new teacher to gradually increase responsibility and participation. (Use and adapt the plan on the "In-Service Training Chart" to meet your needs.)

In-
Service
Training

Full Partnership

The goal of this process is not to have your teacher-in-training take over and teach the entire session alone! At every age level and in every program, children's ministry should always involve at least *two* capable teachers working together to meet the varied needs of the children in the group. This structure is also consistent with quality child safety policies, providing protection for both children and staff. If it is not always possible to achieve this level of staffing, a new staff member should initially be placed in a team situation where the opportunity exists for mutual support.

The most common reason given for not having at least two teachers present in every children's group is that there simply are not enough people who are both capable and willing to serve. The problem is usually phrased as, "If we can barely recruit enough people to have one teacher per group, how would we ever be able to get two?"

However, churches who make a commitment to providing team support in children's ministries soon discover that it is easier to enlist new staff and to retain existing staff when no one is expected to serve alone. As Ecclesiastes 4:9,10 points out, "Two are better than one: . . . If one falls down, his friend can help him up. But pity the man who falls and has no one to help him up!" *(NIV)*.

Usually, one person on a teaching team takes some leadership responsibilities, either due to having more experience, more time available, or more interest and ability for administrative tasks. As a trainer who may no longer be needed as a regular part of the team, you may still offer to periodically meet and help plan the sessions as a way to encourage continued growth. Be sure you model your dependence on the Holy Spirit by praying with your teacher-in-training before each time together.

As the trainer, periodically observe and evaluate the teachers in action. Be sure you offer plenty of affirmation for the things they do well and always offer assistance to help with tasks where improvement is needed. Remember, you want teachers to succeed. At the end of observing a session, give recognition to strong areas and point out one area only that needs improvement. Pray with your teacher-in-training that God's Holy Spirit will continue to teach and guide him through the staff and children of the department in which he has placed the teacher. Be sure to remind both new and experienced teachers of the date of the next training/planning meeting, the telephone numbers of other workers in their department, as well as how to reach you should there be a need.

Chapter Eight

EARLY CHILDHOOD LESSON PLANNING SHEET
(Twos through Fives)

Lesson # _____   Date _____

Quarterly theme: _____   Unit title: _____

Lesson title: _____

Scripture: _____

What student will know: _____

How student will respond: _____

1 Arrival Activities
Materials:

Procedure:

2 Learning Center Activities
1. Purpose:
  Materials:

  Procedure:

2. Purpose:
  Materials:

  Procedure:

3. Purpose:
  Materials:

  Procedure:

4. Purpose:
  Materials:

  Procedure:

3 Bible Story
Materials:

Introduction:

Story:

Application:

4 Follow-up Activities
Materials:

Procedure:

5 Closing Activities
Materials:

Procedure:

ELEMENTARY LESSON PLANNING SHEET
(First through Sixth Grades)

Lesson # _____   Date _____

Quarterly theme: _____   Unit title: _____

Lesson title: _____

Scripture: _____

Memory verse: _____

What student will know: _____

How student will respond: _____

Learning Center Activities	Bible Study Activities	Bible Application Activities
1. Purpose: 　Materials: 　Procedure: **2.** Purpose: 　Materials: 　Procedure: **3.** Purpose: 　Materials: 　Procedure:	Materials: Procedure:	Materials: Procedure:

Closing Activities
Materials:

Procedure:

EARLY CHILDHOOD OBSERVATION SHEET
(Twos through Fives)

Bible story: _____

Lesson aims: _____

Teaching begins the minute each child enters the classroom. How was this time maximized for each child?

List the major sections of the teaching time and how many minutes were devoted to each.

What do you see children doing or saying that shows the lesson aims being accomplished?

How are children involved in learning?

List several classroom management techniques.

How did teachers meet the needs of individual learners?

How were learning styles used?

Comment on the balance of Bible content and application.

What happened to encourage positive relationships?

ELEMENTARY OBSERVATION SHEET
(First through Sixth Grades)

Bible story: _____

Lesson aim: _____

Teaching begins the minute each child enters the classroom. How was this time maximized for each child?

List the major sections of the teaching time and how many minutes were devoted to each.

What do you see children doing or saying that shows the lesson aims being accomplished?

List the ways children were involved in learning.

List several classroom management techniques.

How did teachers use guided conversation during the activities?

How were learning styles accommodated?

Comment on the balance of Bible content and application.

How was the Bible content introduced and then reviewed?

What happened to encourage positive relationships?

IN-SERVICE TRAINING CHART

WEEK		TEACHER-IN-TRAINING		TRAINER
Assist	**Team**	**Early Childhood**	**Children**	
Week 1	Week 1-2	1. Observe the session. Arrive 15 minutes early to see before-class preparations and early-arriver activities. Remain after the session for discussion with workers and trainer.		1. Meet with the teacher-in-training before the session. Explain the basic classroom schedule. 2. Provide a place from which the teacher-in-training may observe. Designate a small group for her to join for small-group times. 3. Answer questions.
	Week 2-4	1. Begin to take part in the session as directed by your trainer. During this time your responsibilities will gradually increase. Continue to assist and observe when you are not leading the teaching time.		1. During these weeks, allow the teacher-in-training to plan and lead specific parts of the session.
Week 2	Week 3	2. Prepare and lead a Bible learning activity.	2. Prepare and lead an entry activity.	2. Gradually increase the teacher-in-training's responsibilities as shown at the left.
	Week 4	3. Prepare and lead a learning activity. Assist with worship and Bible story.	3. Prepare and lead an entry activity. Prepare and lead in application.	
Week 3	Week 5	1. Prepare and lead the Bible story.	1. Prepare and lead the Scripture study. 2. Assist in group worship time.	3. Be sure to: • fully explain the part of the curriculum the teacher-in-training is planning. • be available for discussion after each session. • observe the teacher-in-training, evaluate, and give ideas for areas that need improvement. • make resources available for the part of the session the teacher-in-training is leading.
	Week 6	1. Prepare and lead the Bible story and activity-page time.	1. Prepare and lead the Scripture study. 2. Lead the close of the session.	
Week 4	Week 7-8	1. Plan, prepare, and lead or teach the complete session.		1. Observe and evaluate. 2. Be available to give assistance. 3. Recognize strong points and note only one area per week as needing improvement.

Continuous Training

Focusing on both preservice and in-service training is certainly a strong beginning to meeting the recruitment challenge facing churches today. But ongoing—or *continuous*—training is also a significant solution to the problem.

We all enjoy doing the things we do well. We make firm commitment to those things we value. The tasks that provide us fulfillment are those we continue when we plan how to invest our time and energy. Staff members who enjoy ministry and want to continue doing it are the people who are growing in their skills, character, and spiritual lives. They are people whose ministry efforts have become successful in helping others, fulfilling to themselves, and glorifying and honoring to God. Children's ministry leaders need to help those they recruit to build their skills, strengthen their character, and deepen their spiritual lives. And it will not happen by accident. Leaders must make specific provision for training opportunities that produce those results.

Often when we think of training, the idea of "one more meeting" is not a positive thought. People with today's busy schedules tend to flinch when confronted with another evening away from home. But well-planned meetings executed with care can become happily anticipated events. This chapter provides guidelines for training meetings that include specific skill development, opportunities to plan future lessons, and time focused on personal spiritual growth. Let's begin by answering some important questions.

How Often Should We Meet?

Children's staff members develop an appreciation for productive meetings held once each month, often enough for people to see positive results in their ministry and their own lives. This schedule allows for training in twelve skill areas each year, along with adequate time to address issues of personal growth. Also, monthly meetings encourage teachers to plan lessons for a month at a time. Curriculum is usually organized into units of study with four or five lessons, so planning once a month encourages teachers to plan for a series of lessons that are related to each other in some way.

However, many teachers do not have a history of positive experience with training meetings. The signs are often quite obvious: "We're all so busy!" "You really don't expect us to meet every month, do you?" "I'm happy to teach for awhile, but please don't ask me to come to any meetings." In such cases, a good strategy is to begin one meeting at a time. Start with an important reason for meeting, one that the teachers themselves recognize as having value. If the topic of the meeting addresses needs and concerns of the teachers, they will be likely to attend.

TEACHER TRAINING TONIGHT

One or two successful meetings creates a readiness to accept quarterly meetings, then meetings every other month, and then monthly meetings. Until the response is positive to regularly getting together for training and growth, it is necessary to provide informative and perhaps informal communication between meetings. The goal is to nurture teachers to grow spiritually, to develop godly character traits, to improve their skills, and to encourage their faithfulness. Consider these communication ideas to bridge the time between meetings:

• Mail a summary of key points covered at the meeting, focusing on specific actions that were discussed for teachers to implement. (This is valuable both to refresh the memory of those who attended and to inform those who missed the meeting.)

• Circulate among the staff a video or audio tape that reinforces the main thrust of the meeting. Accompany the tape with a brief response page for each staff member to write down several ideas he or she can put into practice in coming weeks.

• Phone teachers to interact about their efforts to implement ideas from the meeting.

• Form prayer partners within the staff, encouraging them to share requests and praises as they support each other with regular prayer.

• Every other week, e-mail and/or fax a few tips that staff members can use, along with notes of affirmation for things that have been done well. Be sure to include tips for secretaries, greeters, memory work listeners, librarians, and others who provide vital support to teachers.

When Should We Meet?

There is no perfect time, for there will always be conflicts in people's schedules. The specific time that you choose is not as important as the *consistency* of scheduling. Evaluate your church's regular schedule. Survey members. Identify the time when the greatest number of people in your group will be available. It sometimes helps to connect the meetings to a time slot when people already will be at church. This is especially true if a large percentage of your staff live a significant distance from the church.

You may meet Sunday afternoon immediately following morning worship or just before an evening service. Perhaps an evening during the week when there are other activities at the church will work well. There is no "one best time." Become acquainted with the needs and schedules of your people, select a time to meet, and then meet regularly each month at that time. It is helpful for your staff to be able to say, for example, "We always meet the third Sunday afternoon of the month."

There are significant advantages in having all children's teachers meet at the same time, even if they do not all meet together. While there is always the risk that whatever time you select just will not work for some people, setting aside a specific time for children's staff to meet helps to protect that time from other church activities. It also simplifies communication, and allows building a sense of shared ministry among the staff for various age groups. Or you may schedule separate meetings at different times in an attempt to gain maximum participation.

Continuous Training

How Long Should Meetings Be?

One and a half or two hours will provide enough time to explore an area of spiritual growth, to work through a skill-building training session, and to plan for a series of lessons. But how long you meet is not as important as the value and effectiveness of what you do when you do meet.

Who Should Attend?

The size of your church and the number of people involved in ministry to children will help to determine the answer to this question. If the training topic is of interest to those who work with young children as well as those who work with the elementary ages, all staff members can meet together for the spiritual growth and training segments and then separate into age-level groups for planning lessons. A more specific topic, such as "Bible Learning Activities for Ages 2-5," would involve teachers of young children only. In that case, teachers of the elementary ages meeting at the same time could consider another topic. Make sure that training topics are explored from the perspective of support staff as well as that of teachers.

What About Parents?

Occasionally you may wish to include parents in the training portion of a meeting. Topics such as "How People Learn," "Helping Children Learn to Pray," "Dealing with Disruptive Behavior," and "Developing Character in Children" would be appropriate for parents as well as teachers. The program may be continued with only parents after staff members leave to plan lessons, or parents also may be dismissed. In addition to building the skills of parents and staff, this kind of meeting also provides opportunities for parents and staff to build relationships. Including parents in these learning experiences also helps to prepare some of them to consider getting involved in ministry to children besides their own. This can only result in a more meaningful program for children.

Try to include parents in training meetings at least once or twice a year. As this becomes an acceptable plan for your congregation, increase parent involvement to once a quarter.

Do We Need Refreshments?

Fellowship that promotes relationship building is a positive part of training/planning meetings. But the focus does not always need to be on food. Having beverages available (iced tea and soft drinks in warm weather; hot coffee, tea, and cocoa if the weather is cold) can be a good way to help staff feel comfortable, but it is certainly acceptable to meet and share together without beverages or snacks. Some groups may enjoy snacks for special occasions rather than on a regular basis.

If you do want to have refreshments, ask someone who is not a staff member and has no other responsibility for the meeting to prepare simple snacks. Or perhaps parents would enjoy expressing appreciation to teachers of their children in this way.

Where Should We Meet?

Decide the location for your meeting in a way that meets the needs of your specific situation. Some people may prefer a home setting, which may be a bit less formal, but most homes will not accommodate larger groups. Occasionally groups plan to meet in restaurants. If the size of your group is more than ten or twelve, you probably will want to meet in a room at church. If meeting at church, it is often best to not schedule the meeting in the same room(s) where people teach. Meeting in their own classrooms often results in teachers spending time cleaning closets or decorating bulletin boards rather than improving teaching skills or developing personal and spiritual qualities needed for ministry.

Be flexible. The place is less important than what occurs during the meeting.

Should We Provide Child Care?

If child care is a requirement for some staff members, you may wish to make some arrangements to provide it. Again, this will depend on your individual situation and the needs of the majority of staff members. Make sure that in freeing up staff members to attend, the best interests of their children are not overlooked. It is sadly ironic if a meeting focused on ministry to children results in neglecting the children of the participants.

What If Staff Members Don't Want to Come?

Make participation in training/planning meetings a part of the job description that is discussed at the time of recruitment. Point out the value of participation and make it an expected part of each person's commitment right from the beginning. Point out that choir members meet weekly to prepare for their part of the worship service and preparation for teaching is no less important. Meeting for prayer, personal growth, and to develop skills and to plan with others is an integral part of a meaningful Christian education program for children. Such training provides a strong foundation for the individual prayer, planning, and preparation that staff members then do on their own.

In any case, do not let the reluctance of some stop you from providing this valuable resource for others. Avoid the temptation to moan about those who did not come. Instead, rejoice over the ones who attend.

Continuous Training

What Makes a Meeting Meaningful?

Here's a list of guidelines for meaningful meetings. Check the list each time you prepare for a session.

- *Begin on time* no matter who has not arrived.
- *Model the skills* you want teachers to have.
- *Involve participants* in the process. Resist the temptation to lecture extensively. If you really believe what you say about the importance of involvement in the learning process, you will involve teachers in the process of developing skills and planning lessons.
- *Listen* to teachers voice their needs and interests.
- Select topics that will *meet needs* and *build on interests*.
- Use a *variety* of trainers and methods.
- Make certain each session emphasizes practical *application* with the opportunity to practice the skill you are teaching and the character trait you are encouraging.
- *Publicize* the meeting well in advance, even though it is regularly scheduled. Be sure participants are personally reminded of the meeting and aware of the topic.
- Ask staff to make some *preparation* for the meeting. Not only will they benefit from the experience, but they will have greater ownership in the meeting. For example, you might ask people to pray for specific concerns, to read Scripture and curriculum materials related to the lessons they will be planning, to be prepared to teach a new song to the group, or to bring an example of a Bible learning activity that was successful.
- Occasionally provide *recognition* and/or a simple reward for accomplishment: a coupon for yogurt to each one in the department with everyone present, for example, or a bookmark for all who have had an outing with their group of children during the past month.
- *Evaluate* every meeting. Evaluate from a leadership perspective and involve participants in the evaluation too. Prepare a simple evaluation sheet to distribute to a different portion of the group each meeting. Read what is written. Listen to comments. Perhaps the strongest method of evaluation is observation in the classrooms. Are new skills being used? Can you see evidences that staff members are applying information and principles shared at the meetings? Are lessons more effective as a result of planning?

What Topics Should Be Covered?

Survey your staff. Plan topics to meet their needs and answer their questions. Outlines and plans for eleven training/planning meetings to help you begin your continuous training program are suggested in this book. Select topics that will meet current needs of your teachers and answer the questions they are asking now.

You also may identify needs by observing children and teachers in the classroom. Be alert for topics that would be of interest to parents too.

I Can't Do This Alone!

You're right, but don't despair! There are experts in your congregation you can ask to help you. They may not be involved in regular children's ministry but they would be willing to lead a training session. Here are some possibilities:

- *Schoolteacher*: "How People Learn."
- *Nurse or physician*: "Classroom Safety," "Dealing With Emergencies."
- *Counselor*: "Meeting Special Needs."
- *Panel of parents and teachers*: "Developing Acceptable Behavior."

Another type of expert available to help you is the publisher's curriculum consultant. Contact the publisher of the curriculum you use. Often there is someone in your area who can help with topics like organizing materials or lesson planning.

Are There Other Ways to Train Workers?

The answer is an emphatic yes! Consider including these possibilities in your continuous training program:

- *Sunday school conventions*. Investigate. You may discover that there is an annual Sunday school convention held near enough for your teachers to attend.
- *Teacher-training conferences and seminars*. Once again, be alert to opportunities that come to your area. Contact neighboring churches. Plan and work together to promote a training event in your area. Express appreciation to your teachers by providing partial scholarships for registration fees.
- *Develop a resource library*. Notify teachers of specific books and articles that will help them build character, grow spiritually, and develop teaching skills.

How to Use the Sessions Provided in this Book

Beginning on page 67, there are outlines, plans, and reproducible pages for eleven training/planning meetings. The following topics are included.

- Developing Christian Character
- How People Learn
- Lesson Planning
- Dealing With Disruptive Behavior
- Becoming an Effective Teacher
- Building Relationships
- Bible Learning Activities for Ages 2-5
- Bible Learning Activities for Grades 1-6
- Helping Children Learn to Pray
- Helping Children Memorize Scripture
- Family Ministry: Building a Bridge Between Church and Home

Select from this list those that will meet the needs of your staff and schedule them in a sequence that will build on what they already know. Schedule monthly meetings, if possible. If not, begin with quarterly meetings. Study the outlines to become familiar with the concepts they include. Contact individuals who can help you prepare and lead the sessions. Ask participants to be involved in some of the preparation as well.

The plan for each session follows this basic format:

• **Aims**. These are statements of what you want to accomplish. Aims are measurable. Aims deal not only with information (knowledge) but also with response to and application of that knowledge. You may wish to adapt the suggested aims to more specifically meet the needs of your staff. Accomplishment of the aims may be measured partially through observation of workers in the classroom with children.

• **Materials**. Use this list of supplies to help you plan and to help you remember to bring everything needed for the meeting. In some cases, additional resources will be suggested. These are optional, but you may wish to use them if they are available to you.

• **Preparation**. In this section you will find a list of what needs to be done before the meeting, including what to ask participants to do prior to the meeting.

• **Arrival Activities.** Participants will be asked to begin these activities as soon as they arrive. This increases the learning time for those who arrive early, models an effective way to begin a session with children, and helps participants begin to think about and interact with the information and concepts to be considered during the meeting.

• **Exploration Activities.** Participants will interact with the subject matter of the session. You may involve a resource person, use a variety of resources, or lead the discussion yourself. Information to be shared is provided. However, work through it, adapt it, and make it more specific so that it will be of the greatest benefit to your staff. Suggestions for involving participants will be given. Use them! Resist the temptation to lecture.

• **Response and Application.** Participants will be asked to respond to the information they have encountered. Each will select a way to make application of the experience in his or her classroom. Record or share participants' selections in some way. This will encourage accountability to take action.

• **Lesson Planning.** Participants will divide into smaller groups to plan specific lessons. All workers who are teaching the same lesson can meet together. In a church with several workers teaching one age or grade level, each age or grade level can meet together. (For example, all six first-grade teachers or all eight teachers of five-year-olds meet together to plan.)

If you have fewer than three or four people teaching the same lesson, group staff for preschool children together and staff for elementary children together. They may share ideas, support each other in a prayer time, interact about life application emphases, and plan for department functions. Then they can plan for individual lessons at home.

Providing meaningful training/planning meetings is one of the most fulfilling activities a Christian education leader can undertake. By doing so, you enable workers to maintain a level of excitement about their ministry as their skills increase. Recruitment becomes less of a challenge as joyous, fulfilled staff members are willing to renew their commitment to the teaching ministry. Quality learning experiences for children increase as teachers build skills and become more and more excited about their ministries.

Evaluation

The strength of any program is continuous evaluation. The day-to-day responsibilities of guiding a program for children and recruiting and training workers often makes evaluation a low priority. But every part of your program will be enhanced by ongoing and thorough evaluation.

This chapter suggests ways to evaluate the four basic elements of ministry to children: recruitment, training, programming for children, and volunteer staff.

Evaluate Recruitment

Plan to evaluate the effectiveness of your recruitment program once each quarter, or four times a year. Meet with the church leaders to whom you are responsible and discuss these questions:

1. During the past three months, how many people have been individually contacted and asked to participate in some area of children's ministry?

2. How many workers are needed right now to adequately staff programs for children?

3. During the past three months, how many people have accepted responsibilities to become a part of children's ministry?

4. What have we done to communicate children's ministries to our congregation?

5. What have we done to help our congregation develop positive feelings about programs for children?

6. Have we scheduled and planned for an upcoming informational meeting?

7. What one new method will we use this quarter to increase participation in children's ministry?

Evaluate Training

Answer these questions about your training program at least once each quarter, or four times a year:

1. Are we scheduling training and planning meetings on a regular basis?

If your church is not accustomed to training meetings, begin by scheduling one each quarter. After six months to a year, plan for a meeting every other month, then one each month.

2. Are teacher's needs being met at our training meetings?

Talk with teachers about their needs and expectations for the meetings. Plan to build and strengthen skills. Encourage and affirm the ministry that is being accom-

plished. Be sure that the spiritual and character growth and teaching skills being taught and practiced are related to felt needs of teachers.

Meetings need to be well planned and presented, and to begin and end on time. A significant portion of each meeting needs to be invested in planning specific, upcoming lessons. It is important for teachers to discover that their time with their learners is more effective as a result of the time they have invested in training meetings.

3. Are we observing teaching teams being developed? Are relationships among workers being strengthened? Are staff members growing in their spiritual lives, personal character, and teaching skills?

In addition to your own evaluation of the training program, ask teachers to evaluate individual training sessions. Three or four times a year, select a meeting and ask teachers to respond to these questions:

1. What was the most helpful part of this session?
2. How could we improve our training sessions?
3. What topics should we plan to deal with in future meetings?
4. What questions, comments, or suggestions do you have for us to consider when we plan future training meetings?

Evaluate Children's Programming

Sometimes children's ministries provide certain programs for children because "that's the way it has always been." Twice a year, evaluate the programs that form your ministry to children. Are the programs effective? Here are some guidelines for evaluating children's ministry programs.

1. Are we providing a variety of kinds of activity?
2. Are the programs we provide meeting needs of the children in our church and in our community?
3. Do the current programs maintain the interest of the children involved?
4. Can we state the goal for each program? In other words, do we know why we have a club program, a children's choir program, VBS, and summer day camps?
5. Are regular church attenders being challenged?
6. Do newcomers feel comfortable? Can they easily become an active part of the group?
7. Are there enough caring adults to maintain a reasonable ratio of adults to children?
8. Do children have opportunities to participate in meaningful learning experiences?
9. Do children have opportunities to build relationships with caring adults as well as with their peers?
10. Do children experience meaningful worship opportunities?
11. Are children encouraged to be involved in outreach?
12. Is there evidence of spiritual and character growth in the lives of our children?
13. Are we willing to make changes in our programming if our evaluation indicates that change is needed?

Evaluate Workers

We often are fearful of evaluating volunteers. After all, they are volunteering, and besides: what if they decide to quit? But our ministry to children will never succeed unless we see positive results in the lives and ministries of staff members. Is there evidence of spiritual and character growth? Are people demonstrating improvement in their teaching skills? These are questions we must ask to avoid having people just "go through the motions" by filling a position.

Volunteers usually perform to the standards they are given. Be sure that all elements of each job description are carefully described to every individual who is recruited to minister with children.

At the time of recruitment and initial training, let new volunteers know that you will be evaluating on a regular basis. Explain that the goal of your evaluation is always to encourage and help teachers and to insure meaningful learning experiences for all children. Here are some guidelines for evaluating workers.

1. Take care that each new worker understands that every three months you will talk together to determine how things are going with the children.

This regular evaluation helps leaders and recruiters know how effective their recruitment and training is, and it gives workers opportunity to discuss their comfort level in their current assignments.

2. Let workers know that you will be visiting their classrooms to observe on a regular basis.

When you visit, avoid being judgmental and critical. Resist the temptation to sit and take copious notes. Interact with the children as it is appropriate. At the end of the session, point out two or three good things that happened. Affirm and encourage. Mention one thing (if there is one thing) that could be improved. Offer positive suggestions for improvement. Share related resources. Give opportunity for the worker to express feelings and needs or to ask questions.

3. Provide the opportunity for a conference time at church or in the home of the volunteer. Build positive relationships.

4. Send notes of encouragement, pointing out something positive you have observed.

Sometimes your conversations and evaluations with workers will help you and volunteers discover the need for change:

1. Perhaps a different age or grade level will provide a more successful experience for both worker and learners. Make this opportunity a plus, not a failure.

2. Sometimes a change in ministry responsibility is just what the volunteer needs. Some are called to be teachers. Some are wonderful assistants. Some work more comfortably with adults and can become coordinators or superintendents. Some may be skilled in communication and will blossom with the opportunity to develop effective information tools about children's ministry. Not everyone can teach children, but everyone who wants to can be involved in children's ministry in some way. Let evaluation lead to the discovery of the best way for each individual to be a part of this important ministry.

3. From time to time, you will discover a sincere and capable volunteer who should not be working directly with children. Sometimes, but not often, this person is willing

to accept some other task in children's ministry or some other area in the church. We would all prefer to avoid the challenge of asking a teacher to stop teaching, but following these steps will help you find a solution:

- Pray and earnestly seek God's guidance.
- Invest time in observation.
- Make every effort to come to a solution that will improve the situation.
- Meet with the volunteer and another staff person. (Seek the counsel and help of the minister or director of Christian education as necessary.)
- Graciously but honestly discuss the reasons for thinking that a change of ministry is needed.
- You might ask the volunteer to tell what he or she finds difficult about this ministry.
- Be a careful listener.
- Suggest other areas of ministry that will be more suitable for the volunteer. Follow up to insure that the worker is placed in a suitable and worthwhile position of service.
- Express appreciation for the effort and time given to children's ministry.
- Continue to show interest in and concern for the individual volunteer.

Evaluation

Resources

The first step in recruiting is to take good care of the volunteers you already have. These books will provide insight and help in addition to the ideas in chapter 6.

Inviting Volunteers to Minister, John Cionca (Standard Publishing, 1999)
Treat 'Em Right, Susan Cutshall (Standard Publishing, 1999)
Awesome Volunteers, Christine Yount (Group, 1998)

The following resources can help you develop plans for preservice training.

Teacher Training Series, Karyn Henley (Standard Publishing, 1997)
    Learning Centers
    Young Children: What Are They Like?
    Play: Building Relationships
    Time Management for Teachers
    Parents: Teaching Partners
    Communicating With Young Children
    Behavior Management
    Learning Strengths
    Scripture Memory
    Storytelling
Child-Sensitive Teaching, Karyn Henley (Standard Publishing, 1997)
The 21st Century Sunday School, Wes Haystead (Standard Publishing, 1995)
The Last-Minute Sunday School Teacher, Cliff Schimmels (Standard Publishing, 1998)
Quick Relief for Sunday School Teachers (Group, 1998)

To enrich the training sessions, try some of the supplementary information in the following publications. Display the books at appropriate training sessions to help workers know what is available.

200+ Activities for Children's Ministry, Susan Lingo (Standard Publishing, 1999)
Act It Out!, Randy Ritz (Standard Publishing, 1999)
Bible Crafts & More for Ages 2–4 (Standard Publishing, 1999)
Bible Crafts & More for Ages 4–8, Nancy I. Sanders (Standard Publishing, 1999)
Bible Message Make-n-Takes, Susan Lingo (Standard Publishing, 1998)
Bulletin Boards for Children's Ministry, Mary Tucker (Standard Publishing, 1999)
Celebrate! A Holiday Handbook, Patricia Alderdice Senseman (Standard Publishing, 1998)

Classroom Discipline Made Easy, Barbara Bolton (Standard Publishing, 1997)
Creative Bible Games for All Ages, Judy Dorsett (Standard Publishing, 1998)
Creative Bible Learning: Arts & Crafts, Karyn Henley (Standard Publishing, 1998)
Creative Bible Learning: Science & Cooking, Karyn Henley (Standard Publishing, 1998)
Creative Bible Learning: Story Telling, Karyn Henley (Standard Publishing, 1998)
Handbook of Bible Festivals, Galen Peterson (Standard Publishing, 1996)
Helping Kids Through Tough Times, Doris Sanford (Standard Publishing, 1995)
Kids-Tell-'Em Bible Stories, Susan Lingo (Standard Publishing, 1999)
Larger-Than-Life Activities, Susan Lingo (Standard Publishing, 1997)
Parent Connection, Karin Klein (Standard Publishing, 1995)
Teaching Our Children to Pray, Susan Lingo (Standard Publishing, 1995)

Video training resources are available for use in addition to or instead of the training sessions offered in this book. For more information, ask for the *Design for Teaching Videos* (Standard Publishing).

Host a *Building Character Training Seminar* sponsored by Children of the World, Campus Crusade for Christ's Ministry to Children, directed by Vernie Schorr. For information contact Children of the World, 30981 Via Estenaga, San Juan Capistrano, CA 92675.

Training Sessions

Outlines and plans for eleven training/planning sessions are included in this section to help you begin your continuous training program.

DEVELOPING CHRISTIAN CHARACTER
(1 ½–2 hours)

Aims
During this training session, each participant may:
- Identify the need for character building emphasis and integration.
- Become aware of eight foundational virtues.
- Explore ways to integrate these eight virtues with Bible stories and learning activities.
- Utilize ten big ideas on developing character in planning specific lessons and events for children.

Materials
Name tags
Blank sheets of 8 ½" by 11" white paper
Pencils
Photocopies of page 71
Cups and peanuts
Poster board or transparencies
transparency pens or markers
overhead projector (optional)

Preparation
Photocopy the response sheet on page 71 for each participant.
Prepare visuals as described:

1. A transparency or poster divided into eight boxes, in each of which you letter a personal quality/idea/value you want to develop or continue to develop for yourself. For example: responsible, encouraging, enjoy music.

2. Another transparency or poster divided into eight boxes. Letter these eight virtues: Compassion, Forgiveness, Integrity, Respect, Responsibility, Initiative, Cooperation, Perseverance.

3. Another transparency or poster titled "Three Approaches to Developing Character." Add three subpoints: 1. Model/Example; 2. Choice/Conflict; 3. Intentional Strategies.

4. Letter these game directions on a transparency or poster:

responsibility	encouraging
enjoy music	integrity
creativity	truthfulness
patience	grace

0-1: Give a peanut to the person on your right.
2-3: Give a peanut to the youngest person.
4-5: Give a peanut to the person on your left.
6-7: Give a peanut to anyone you choose.
8-9: Ask the person on your left to give a peanut to the person on your right.
10-11: Don't give a peanut away.
12-13: Eat one peanut.
14-15: Choose a person who can eat one peanut.

Arrival Activities (arrival plus 3-5 minutes)

1. Put on name tags to assist participants in getting acquainted.
2. Ask each person to talk with a partner about a time in his childhood when a significant adult required him to be a person of high moral character.

Exploration Activities (25-30 minutes)

Our goal in this session is to think and plan ways to intentionally build godly character in the lives of children. It is important to first identify some of the ideas, values, and beliefs we presently hold. Think about some ideas you wish to pass on to others. What are some personal character virtues you hold for yourself? To help you think about your ideas more concretely, use a piece of blank paper.

Guide everyone in folding a sheet of 8 1/2" by 11" paper four times, three times horizontally, then once vertically, making eight sections.

In each section write a personal quality, idea, or value you want to develop or continue to develop for yourself. You have about three minutes to complete this task. *After a minute or two, show the transparency or poster you prepared.* Here are some of my ideas that may stimulate your thinking.

Allow another minute of work. Then instruct the participants to tear their page into eight rectangles and place the eight pieces in the order of importance to them. Number 1 is the most important. Allow 3 minutes, then ask participants to choose partners and share the ideas they placed as number 1 and number 2, telling why they chose them. Allow 5 minutes.

By putting these qualities in the order of importance, and sharing your reasons for your choices, you have indicated some of the ideology, philosophy, theology, character, values, and ethics that you hold.

Eight Foundational Virtues: Show the second transparency or poster you prepared. Here are eight character virtues, all based on God's character. They are foundational in the development of godly character, as other character virtues and traits grow from them. *Distribute photocopies of page 71.*

For example, *compassion* is sympathy for someone else's suffering or misfortune, together with the desire to help. It includes love, care, kindness, commitment, and acceptance of self and others. Similarly, *forgiveness* means to stop blaming or feeling anger toward someone who has hurt or wronged us; to pardon or excuse a wrong thought or action. It includes the virtues of humility, joy, and peace.

These virtues are all connected, and specific traits develop and grow out of more than one foundational virtue. For example, obedience develops from compassion, respect, and responsibility. Our goal in this session is not to analyze and evaluate the definitions and connections of these virtues. Our focus is on how we can effectively develop these traits in the minds and spirits of children.

Approaches to Developing Character: Show "Three Approaches" transparency or poster. Here are three approaches to developing character. Let's consider the first, Model/Example. More character is developed as it is "caught," rather than "taught." The character displayed by others in everyday experiences significantly influences children's character. Read what the response sheet says about *respect*, then tell your partner one way you can model respect in your class or home next week. Be specific. You have two minutes.

Read aloud this statement: Respect is not consistently given unless it is consistently received. *Ask:* What experiences have you had with respect or lack of respect that support this statement? *Allow three minutes for participants to share their thoughts.*

The second way to develop character is through Choice/Conflict. Teachers can guide the development of positive Christ-like character by using moments of decision, helping a child make the best choice, or learn from having made a poor choice. Helping a child solve a real problem at the moment it occurs is one of the most effective learning experiences. These are called "teachable moments." Let's look at four skills to help you use teachable moments to guide children to learn to solve problems. *List these points on the chalkboard or a blank transparency.*

1. Accept feelings.
2. Affirm.
3. Clarify.
4. Guide.

Listen to four examples of teacher conversation as I read them aloud. After each example, we'll have a minute or two to identify how that skill is helpful for a child facing a decision.

1. Accept feelings: "I can tell you are angry. The two of you sit here and take three deep breaths and then we will talk."
2. Affirm: "I know you can make this choice. You may need some more information to make a choice."
3. Clarify: "Stefani, what did you see happen with the green pencil?"
4. Guide: "What might you have done differently? What would be better the next time that happens?"

The third approach to teaching character is Intentional Strategies. There is always a need for structured, planned teaching experiences. This involves determining what character trait you wish to emphasize, usually one that is illustrated in a current lesson or series of lessons. Then identify measurable objectives and strategies to teach that character trait.

For example, in teaching the virtue of responsibility, you could give children opportunities to:
• Talk about good and bad experiences of the day or week. (Looking back on something they wish they had done differently can be helpful in creating an open climate.)
• Handle money or other resources for specific purposes.
• Have a special place for personal belongings.
• Borrow, use, and return items with permission.
• Complete tasks in a mutually agreeable manner and time.

As children begin to demonstrate a virtue, it is important to label their actions and give approval. For example, what are some evidences of responsibility for which children should be given approval? *List group members' ideas on the chalkboard or a blank transparency. For example:*

- Telling the truth.
- Completing tasks.
- Handling money or other resources properly.
- Caring for the property of others and their own.
- Being on time.
- Adjusting personal desires for the benefit of another.

Response and Application (3-5 minutes)

Games may be used to give children first-hand experience with character traits. We are going to learn and play a game to build the character trait of responsibility with the actions of giving and receiving. *Ask the participants to form trios. Distribute peanuts in cups, instructing each person to take four peanuts. In each trio, players hold four peanuts in one hand and make a fist with the other hand. As one player counts, players in unison pat fists on knees three times. On the third path, each player extends zero to five fingers. The player who counted aloud counts the total fingers showing in that trio, then follows the Game Directions poster or transparency. Repeat with players taking turns counting. Play until time is called (three to five minutes) or one person has no peanuts left. Then guide the group in responding to these questions for another three to five minutes:*

1. Was it more fun to give or to receive?
2. How does it feel to take a person's last peanut?
3. How does it feel to give away your last peanut?
4. What character traits were practiced or taught in this game?
5. How would this game build a child's character?

Lesson Planning (50-60 minutes)

Next you will be able to plan in your teaching teams or work on individual lesson plans for the next unit of lessons in your curriculum. You need your curriculum, your response sheet from this session, and blank lesson planning sheets (pages 46 and 47). As you work, be sure to make some intentional plan for integrating one of the eight foundational character virtues into each lesson. When possible, choose a virtue that can be emphasized throughout your ministry or church.

In addition to planning lessons, invest some time in praying together. Share your prayer concerns for each other as well as for individual children and their families. Ask God to protect us and keep us a staff of people who seek to honor God by developing godly character in our own lives and the lives of the children we teach.

Note: The remaining sessions include the option to integrate one of the foundational character virtues.

Training Sessions

CHARACTER BUILDING

Foundational Virtues

Compassion is sympathy for someone else's problems, together with the desire to help. It includes love, care, kindness, commitment, and acceptance of self and others.

Forgiveness means to stop blaming someone who has hurt or wronged us; to pardon or excuse a wrong thought or action. Forgiveness breaks the cycle of revenge.

Integrity is utter sincerity and honesty. It includes truth, discernment, keeping promises, and building security.

Respect is showing honor to other people by listening and being courteous. It includes self-respect along with respect for authority.

Responsibility means personally accepting accountability for behavior, thoughts, choices, and speech.

Initiative is choosing to take the first step in thinking, doing, or learning, demonstrating responsible thoughts and actions without prompting or outside influences. It includes taking responsibility for follow-through of what has begun.

Cooperation is willingly working together to reach a common goal.

Perseverance is a continual, steady effort made to fulfill some goal, task, or commitment; to persist in spite of difficulties, opposition, or discouragement.

Ten Big Ideas on Developing Character

1. Children develop character slowly and in stages.
2. Respect children and require respect in return.
3. Teach and develop character by example.
4. Help children learn to think honestly.
5. Help children assume real responsibilities
6. Balance high support and high control.
7. Initiate and demonstrate forgiveness, regardless of blame.
8. Love children! Love is vital for character development.
9. Provide ways for children to make choices.
10. Ask questions instead of giving answers.

HOW PEOPLE LEARN
(1 ½–2 hours)

Aims
During this training session, each participant may:
- Discover three ways people learn.
- Identify ways for learners to involve all five senses in a variety of Bible learning activities.
- Explore the implications of choice and variety in the learning process.
- Utilize these principles in planning a specific lesson or lessons.
- **Option:** Identify the integration of the character virtue *respect*.

Materials
Bibles
Curriculum
Name tags (if needed)
Photocopies of page 75
Pencils
Lesson planning sheets
Overhead transparencies or poster board
Overhead projector (optional)
Transparency pens or markers
Index cards
Envelopes

Preparation
1. Invite staff members and ask them to bring current curriculum to the meeting.
2. Letter 2-4 sets of index cards (one word per card) as shown in the sketch.

TO	LEARN	YOU	MUST

3. Scramble each set of cards. Place each set in an envelope with these instructions on the envelope: "Arrange words in the correct order. Discuss the statement in relation to how people learn."
4. Make a photocopy of page 75 for each participant.
5. Make photocopies of lesson planning sheets. (See pages 46 and 47.) Each person needs one for each lesson in the coming month or unit.
6. Prepare overhead transparencies or posters of "Ways People Learn." See the illustration.
7. If participants need name tags to become better acquainted, place these near the door.
8. **Option:** Display the word *respect* on a large poster.

Training Sessions

Arrival Activities (arrival plus 3-5 minutes)

1. Put on name tags to assist participants in getting acquainted.

2. Ask participants to unscramble and discuss the two statements in the envelopes with two or three other people.

3. Have participants to sit in groups according to the age or grade they teach. Guide individuals in the group to tell the others about the best or most encouraging thing that happened the last time they taught.

4. Distribute photocopies of page 75. Provide pencils as needed.

Exploration Activities/Response and Application (25–30 minutes)

We are going to discover some ideas about the ways people learn. When you entered the room, some of you unscrambled two sentences that state two important ideas about learning. *Ask participants to tell what the sentences are.* How can we motivate our students to want to learn? *Accept and affirm participants' responses, involve the learners, help learners make meaningful application, respect individual differences, interests, learning styles.* What are some ways you have been able to "make learning a joy?" *Ask participants to discuss this question in their small groups.* Complete the first sentence on your response sheet by writing one new idea for making learning a joy.

It is helpful for us to identify three learning styles that are present in all of our children's classrooms. Most children (and adults) learn through more than one learning style, although they usually prefer one above the others. Learning is more efficient when we use the learner's dominant style.

Some are visual learners. *Refer to transparency or poster.* Others are auditory learners. Still others are kinesthetic "hands on" or tactile learners. It is impossible to include all three learning styles every minute of every class session. However, opportunities to learn visually, auditorily, and kinesthetically should be provided at some point during every class session. By providing for varied approaches to learning, we give individual respect and increase learning.

For the next six to seven minutes, share with others in your group about ways you can meet the needs of these three kinds of learners. Share several examples of activities for visual learners, auditory learners, and kinesthetic learners. What activities involve children in seeing? What will they be doing to use listening or hearing to learn? How will they be involved in "hands-on" activities? During your small-group discussion time, write ideas in the spaces provided on your response sheets. *Circulate through the room, encouraging participants to focus on the questions and record ideas on the response sheets.*

One effective way to provide for all three kinds of learners is to offer a choice of various meaningful activities. Children will select the activity that will provide the most meaningful learning experience for them. They will not identify the activity as a *visual* activity. However, they will select the activity that is the most comfortable for them. Children tend to participate in the activity that enables them to achieve the most efficient learning possible.

Teachers, your task is to provide activities that include all learning styles and then to

> **Ways People Learn:**
>
> Visual
>
> AUDITORY
>
> KINESTHETIC

structure your class time so that children can choose from your carefully-planned activities. In just a few minutes, you will have the opportunity to make lesson plans that will implement this concept.

Consideration of the five senses can easily become part of the criteria by which you plan activities and methods to use. Children come to us with all five senses. Most class periods involve seeing and hearing but neglect the other three senses. Yet many times we do have opportunities to use smell, touch, and taste in the learning experiences we plan. It is not always possible to use all five senses, but we need to be alert to lessons that can be made more meaningful by using an increased number of senses.

At the bottom of your response sheet, you will see a list of the five senses and a place to check if you know which ones you will plan to use during your next class session. Please complete this section of the response sheet during your planning time.

Lesson Planning (50–80 minutes)

"For the next _____ minutes, please work in your teaching teams. *If you do not have teaching teams, teachers can work on individual lesson plans.* Make your plans for the next unit of lessons in our curriculum. You will need your curriculum, your response sheets, and lesson-planning sheets.

Refer to your response sheets as you work. be sure to include some visual, auditory, and kinesthetic activities in each class session. Also provide opportunities to use all five senses.

In addition to planning lessons, invest some time in praying together. Share your prayer concerns. Pray for individual children and their families. Ask God to give you insights as you plan for the learning experiences that will meet the needs of your learners. Thank God for using you in a ministry that will contribute to the lives of children; they are of great value to God!

Note: If you are providing refreshments, this might be a good time for a short break to allow time for participants to select a snack and take it to their planning area. Participants may move to their classrooms to plan or may group themselves in various sections of the room you have been using for the first part of the meeting.

Option: Just before you move to your planning areas, what is the character virtue I integrated into this training time? (Respect.) As you plan, look for ways to integrate a character virtue into each of your sessions.

Training Sessions

HOW PEOPLE LEARN

In order to make learning a joy, I will

Needs of visual learners in my class are met when

Needs of auditory learners in my class are met when

Needs of kinesthetic learners in my class are met when

Check (✔) each of the five senses you will use in
your next class session. Write or tell someone what
you will do.

❑ See _____

_____

❑ Hear _____

_____

❑ Smell _____

_____

❑ Touch _____

_____

❑ Taste _____

_____

LESSON PLANNING
(1 ½–2 hours)

Aims
During this training session, each participant may:
- Discover the advantages of planning with a partner or a team.
- Experience an effective planning meeting.
- Make a commitment to investing time and effort in thorough lesson planning.
- **Option:** Identify the integration of the character virtue *perseverance*.

Materials
Bibles
Curriculum
Name tags (if needed)
Photocopies of page 79
Pencils
Lesson planning sheets
Overhead transparencies or poster board
Overhead projector (optional)
Transparency pens or markers
Highlighter markers

Preparation
1. Prepare name tags, if needed for your participants to become acquainted with each other.
2. Remind workers to bring their curriculum.
3. Make a photocopy of page 79 for each participant.
4. Make photocopies of lesson planning sheets. (See pages 46 and 47.) Each staff member needs one for each lesson in the coming month or unit.
5. Make overhead transparencies or posters.
6. **Option:** Display the word *perseverance*.

Arrival Activities (arrival plus 3-5 minutes)
1. Ask participants to put on nametags if you plan to use them.
2. Display a transparency or poster with these directions:

> WELCOME! Please do the following:
> 1. Introduce yourself to at least one person you do not know.
> 2. Sit with others who serve in your department. (*Or* who teach the same lesson you teach.)
> 3. Talk about your greatest challenge related to lesson planning.

Training Sessions

Exploration Activities (15-20 minutes)

As we begin to think about the importance of lesson planning to our teaching ministry, let's think about the words of Paul in 2 Timothy 3:16, 17: "All Scripture is God-breathed and is useful for teaching, rebuking, correcting and training in righteousness, so that the man of God may be thoroughly equipped for every good work" (*NIV*).

Our primary aim is to enable children to know God, to accept His great gift of salvation, and then to know and apply His Word so well that their attitudes and actions will increasingly reflect God's character. God's Word must become the practical measure that is at the heart of daily decisions. Eventually our goal for our students would be "Do your best to present yourself to God as one approved, a workman who does not need to be ashamed and who correctly handles the word of truth" (2 Timothy 2:15, *NIV*).

We know that God's Word is able to become the guiding force in the lives of our students. However, learning experiences that are not thoroughly planned can certainly slow down the process. Our desire is to plan and prepare so carefully that the teaching/learning experience will contribute to significant growth in the lives of our students. An added benefit to this process will be that teachers grow too. Effective, consistent lesson planning takes perseverance.

Never, never give up planning your lessons. One of the purposes of our time together today (tonight) is to provide opportunity for careful lesson planning. Along with opportunity to plan lessons, we try to help each other develop and strengthen teaching skills. Our focus for this training session is lesson planning.

Distribute the photocopies of page 79. You may also want to prepare a transparency or poster to match the response sheet. We want to keep our guidelines as simple as possible and at the same time develop a procedure for lesson planning that is effective.

Guideline number one is **"Pray throughout the planning process."** Please fill this in on the response sheet. Pray that God will give you insights about the Scripture you are teaching. Pray that he will work in the lives of your students during the week. Pray for special needs of the children in your class. Ask God to help you live out concepts in the Scripture. Pray for other teachers. Invest in each other as you form a team to minister to children.

"Strengthen your teaching skills and your character" is guideline number two. Regularly work on strengthening or developing teaching skills. One of the purposes of our regular meetings is to focus on a skill. Today it is lesson planning. At the same time, it is vital that we give the same level of attention to our own personal, spiritual growth, seeking to develop godly character in our lives. Thus, in this session, *perseverance* is the virtue you will notice I am emphasizing.

Guideline number three is **"Prepare a written planning sheet."** Parts of the sheet may be completed when you plan with others and parts will be completed individually. There is no substitute for careful and thorough planning. The investment of some time each day in planning will reap the benefit of a well-executed class session that meets the needs of the children and that shares God's Word effectively.

You will notice that below the spaces for the three guidelines are seven columns. These may be used to develop a weekly lesson-planning sequence. Planning that uses some time each day will be more effective than several hours spent in planning and preparation on Saturday. This chart is organized for those who work with children on Sunday. If you are part of a children's program that meets on another day, just shift the names of the days so that your chart begins and ends with the day you meet with your group of children.

Response Activities (10-15 minutes)

For the next ten to fifteen minutes, read through the items listed for each day. Using a highlighter marker, highlight each statement that is something you plan to do. Shift items from day to day to fit your schedule better. Please be sure there is something you plan to do each day. Then add any other items you would like to make a part of your lesson-planning sequence.

Work individually for a few minutes, and then share some of your ideas with others in your group. Make an effort to share things you see in this planning procedure that will help to meet the challenge you identified earlier. For example, if you said that your planning challenge is having enough time to do it, perhaps dividing the planning steps between seven days will help you meet that time challenge.

Lesson Planning (50-80 minutes)

For the rest of our time together, you will actually work to plan some lessons you will be teaching during the next few weeks. *Be sure each staff member has an adequate supply of planning sheets. You may wish to distribute more than will be needed so that individuals could begin to work on the next group of lessons whenever it is convenient.* Work in your teaching teams to plan for the next four or five weeks. Be sure to plan all segments of each section that you will be doing together as a team. You may complete some of the individual sections at home.

Please begin your planning time by praying for each other and for your learners. Share ideas and resources.

Option: Identify the character virtue you will integrate into your lessons. Choose from the following: compassion, forgiveness, integrity, respect, responsibility, initiative, cooperation, perseverance. As you plan these lessons, focus on helping children discover ways to apply the Scripture in their daily lives, developing the virtue you selected to emphasize.

Training Sessions

LESSON PLANNING

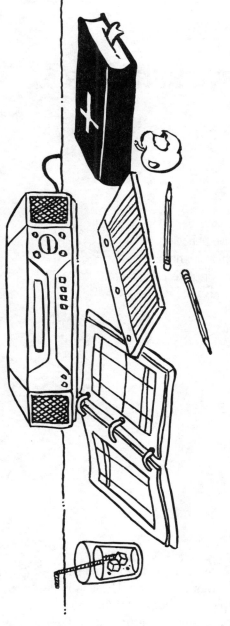

Guidelines for Planning:

1. _____

2. _____

3. _____

Sunday	Monday	Tuesday	Wednesday	Thursday	Friday	Saturday
• pray • Evaluate Lesson • Read Scripture • Define life application/ virtue to emphasize • Mail cards, etc.	• pray • Read curriculum • Complete plan sheet	• pray • Select activities • List supplies • Outline story	• pray • Gather/prepare materials • phone follow-up	• pray • practice Bible story • Use activity materials that are new to you	• pray • Write guided conversation ideas • Read Scripture • Review curriculum	• pray • Double-check supplies • Retell story • practice using visuals • Load car • Sleep well!

DEALING WITH DISRUPTIVE BEHAVIOR
(1 ½–2 hours)

Aims
During this training session, each participant may
- Identify specific disruptive behaviors.
- Interact with a panel on ways to deal with disruptive behavior.
- Plan a strategy that will help to prevent disruptive behavior.
- Develop a strategy to respond to disruptive behavior when it occurs.
- **Option:** Identify the integration of the character virtue *responsibility*.

Materials
Bibles
Curriculum
Name tags (if needed)
Photocopies of page 83
Transparency pens or markers
Pencils
Index cards
Lesson planning sheets
Overhead transparency or poster board
Overhead projector (optional)

Preparation
1. Several weeks before the meeting, invite four or five individuals to be part of a panel that will facilitate a discussion of disruptive behavior of children. These individuals may be parents, teachers, or other staff. Assure panel members that they do not need to be experts; they just need to be willing to share ideas and experiences. Their role is to stimulate thinking and to encourage staff and possibly parents.

2. This would be an appropriate meeting for parents. Consider inviting them to join their children's teachers to discuss this important topic.

3. If parents are invited, this may be an appropriate meeting to have a light snack. Enlist a "snack person" to plan and provide it.

4. Make photocopies of page 83.

5. Prepare an overhead transparency or poster of page 83.

6. Place name tags and pens near the door. Place a response sheet and an index card on every chair.

7. **Option:** Display the word *responsibility*.

Training
Sessions

Arrival Activities (arrival plus 3-5 minutes)

1. Ask each participant to make and wear a nametag.

2. Ask participants to identify the most disruptive behavior in their classrooms and write it on an index cards. Collect the cards. If parents are participating, ask them to write the most disruptive behavior that occurs at home.

3. Remove duplicates. Give the cards to the panel to read before they interact with the group. They may wish to decide who will respond to which behavior.

Exploration Activities (25-30 minutes)

We have taken the first step to an effective, responsible approach to disruptive behavior by changing our vocabulary. We made the change from saying 'discipline problem,' to the term 'behavior challenge.' This simple change in terminology helps us to develop a more positive and responsible attitude toward disruptive behavior. A positive attitude is the first step to successful behavior management.

Our second step is to remember that our goal is to help children develop self-discipline, to become responsible for their own choices and actions. This begins to happen as our positive attitude helps us plan for ways to meet needs of children and avoid or prevent behavior challenges.

Third, here's a valuable tip: Listen to behavior! The behavior of a child communicates a message to us. Sometimes it is saying, "Hey, look at me! I need your attention!" Or it may say, "I just can't sit still this long." Or "I don't understand what you want me to do." Listen and respond! 1 Corinthians 13:4-7 gives guidelines for an appropriate response. *Read the verses from an easy-to-understand translation.*

Just before our panel comes to respond to the behaviors you described earlier, let's look at the response sheet and prepare two lists. One is to help us prevent behavior challenges, and the other is to provide some tips for when we need to respond to challenging behavior. *Encourage participants to write on their response sheets the following statements in **boldface type** as you add them to the overhead transparency or poster you have prepared.*

Prevent

1. **Involve learners in age-appropriate and meaningful activities.** Children who are involved in meaningful activities that are appropriate for their age level and reinforce the concepts being learned usually do not present challenging behavior.

2. **Set realistic standards for behavior.** Consider age-appropriate standards. Know the attention span of your learners. Be aware of the areas and stages of child development.

3. **Plan and provide for a change of pace.** Provide for a change of pace during the session. Children need some quiet activities and some active activities. They need to work individually or in small groups for most of the time. Minimize large-group activities.

4. **Provide an environment that is appropriate and affirming.** Develop a room environment that is conducive to learning. Try to provide the correct size of furniture and equipment. Be certain that the emotional environment is positive. Value and affirm each child. Encourage children to be responsible for cleaning their room and caring for materials.

5. **Plan and prepare the lesson thoroughly.** Be sure that your lesson planning and

preparation are thorough. A well-prepared lesson is the best insurance against disruptive behavior.

Even though you utilize every suggestion for preventing behavior challenges, occasionally you will be faced with disruptive behavior. Here are some steps to take that will deal with negative behavior in a positive and effective way.

The child who is displaying challenging behavior needs to know specifically what behavior is not permitted, why it will not be accepted, and what action is responsible and acceptable. Then expect the child to accept the consequence of his actions.

Respond
1. **Talk with the child individually if possible.**
2. **Ask the child to explain what happened.**
3. **Explain why that action cannot continue.**
4. **Allow the child to experience the consequence.** For example, if he throws blocks, he must leave the block area.
5. **Redirect the child to an acceptable and responsible behavior.**

For the next fifteen minutes or so, let's interact with our panel as they respond to your questions. Refer to the "Prevent" And "Respond" columns of your response sheet and notice how these ten suggestions are referred to by members of the panel. *Ask the panel to respond to the behaviors written on the index cards.*

Response/Application (15 minutes)
Look at the spaces at the bottom of your response sheet. There are eight blanks, with a shorter line in front of each one. On the longer blanks, list challenging behaviors in your class or home. On the shorter lines, write the number of the prevent and/or response tips you will take in order to meet that challenge.

Please turn to the person sitting next to you and pray together. Ask God to help you be consistent in the way you help children change behavior patterns.

Lesson Planning (35-65 minutes)
Since meeting behavior challenges is usually a strongly-felt need among teachers (and parents), there will be less time devoted to lesson planning at this training session. No doubt the discussion will fill much of the time available.

Encourage teachers to plan all of what they need to consider together for each of the lessons in the upcoming month or unit, looking for ways to integrate and emphasize a Christian virtue that is illustrated in the Bible content. Then use any remaining time for more specific planning and prayer, with a focus on planning to reduce behavior challenges. Utilize the principles shared earlier in the session.

Training Sessions

DEALING WITH DISRUPTIVE BEHAVIOR

prevent

P-1.

P-2.

P-3.

P-4.

P-5.

_____ _____

_____ _____

_____ _____

_____ _____

RESPOND

R-1.

R-2.

R-3.

R-4

R-5.

_____ _____

_____ _____

_____ _____

_____ _____

BECOMING AN EFFECTIVE TEACHER
(1 ½–2 hours)

Aims
During this training session, each participant may
- Identify four characteristics of an effective teacher.
- Self-evaluate in relationship to these characteristics.
- Develop an individual plan to strengthen these four characteristics as needed.
- **Option:** Identify the integration of the character virtue *compassion.*

Materials
Bibles
Lesson planning sheets
Curriculum
Camera
Film
Bookmarks
Large sheets of shelf paper or newsprint (about 3 by 4 feet)
Name tags (if needed)
Cassette of your choice
Cassette player
Photocopies of page 87
Pencils

Preparation
1. Several weeks before the meeting, visit classrooms and take photographs of teachers and children in action. Mount them on poster board or a bulletin board in the room where you will be meeting.

2. Remind workers to bring their curriculum. Send each one a simple bookmark on which you have lettered "You Are SPECIAL!"

3. Select a cassette of encouraging, uplifting Christian music to play in the background while participants are arriving.

4. Make a photocopy of page 87 for each participant.

5. Make photocopies of lesson-planning sheets (pages 46 and 47).

6. Prepare two sheets of shelf paper or newsprint. Write one of these phrases at the top of each one:

    An effective teacher is . . .

    An effective teacher needs . . .

7. Attach the paper to walls or place on tables. Place markers nearby.

8. **Option:** Display the word *compassion.*

Training Sessions

Arrival Activities (arrival plus 3-5 minutes)

Direct participants to respond to the two unfinished sentences you have lettered on sheets of paper. They may write words or sketch pictures to complete the sentences.

Exploration Activities (15-20 minutes)

If each of us was asked the following question, we would all answer with a resounding yes: "Do you want to be an effective teacher?"

We are serious about serving God through ministry to children. We understand the importance of sharing God's Word effectively. We are anxious to do our best in all of our endeavors. It's easy to answer yes. But how can we increase our effectiveness? After all, we are all busy people. We don't have several hours a week to work on improving skills in order to become more effective. But skill building is only one part of effective teaching.

Tonight (today) we will have an opportunity to identify four characteristics of an effective teacher. There are many more than four, but a careful focus on four will be more beneficial than a long list of characteristics.

To begin our discussion, let's read some of your responses to the incomplete sentences on the large sheets of paper. I think you will discover that our four characteristics will include some of the items you added to these sentences. *Ask two or three people to read the responses.*

Distribute the response sheets. Look at the four boxes on your response sheets. We will fill in the blanks in each one to identify the characteristics.

Work together with three or four people to discover these four characteristics. *Allow three to four minutes for this activity and then help as needed to identify the four characteristics.*

Answers:

1. Grows spiritually and in character.
2. Plans and prepares well.
3. Builds relationships.
4. Helps learners apply Scripture.

Individually rate yourself on a scale of 1-10 (10 being the strongest) on each of these four characteristics.

Growing spiritually and in character is the beginning of teaching effectively. Each of us needs to invest time in strengthening our relationship with God. He desires our fellowship. Psalm 46:10 reminds us, "Be still, and know that I am God" (*NIV*). Do we find time each day to "be still?" Do we read Scripture, meditate on Scripture, plan specifically to make application of Scripture in our daily lives? Do we praise God through prayer? Do we seek his direction and guidance in the decision-making process? Spiritual growth occurs when we intentionally plan to invest time and energy regularly in developing a close and meaningful relationship with God. Are we truly committed to being people of high moral character? Do we actively seek to do the right thing, the right way, for the right reason? Do we strive to benefit others and glorify God in obedience to his Word?

Planning and preparing well is a part of what we are doing when we meet here together. We have been discovering that a well-planned lesson is one that maintains the interest of our children. It allows us to feel confident that we are ready to interact with children in meaningful ways. Activities will meet the needs of our learners. Team and individual planning will insure meaningful learning experiences.

Building relationships with our learners requires an investment of time and energy. Remember for a moment teachers you had when you were a child. Think about those who had a significant impact on your life. Without a doubt they are the ones who were compassionate and cared enough to build a relationship with you. Plan an outing with your learners once or twice a year; perhaps you can even manage to have one each quarter! Simplicity is important. The crucial factor is being together and demonstrating love, care, and kindness in addition to time spent in the classroom. The event itself does not need to be elaborate. It can be as simple as taking lunch to church and eating together after the morning service. It can be taking a walk through a park, picking up litter. Be creative and enjoy the time together.

Helping learners apply Scripture at some time during each learning experience is essential. Plan specifically for activities that stress application. Help learners plan for application at school and at home during the week. Discuss their progress next week. Build in accountability.

Response and Application (10 minutes)

Now it's time for us to apply the concepts we have been exploring. Look at the bottom of your response sheet. You will see a piece of stationery. Write a letter to yourself with reminders of actions you will take to grow in one or more of these four areas of effective teaching. Be sure to include compassion towards yourself and others.

Use about five minutes to write your letter. Then share one thing you wrote with another person. Ask your neighbor to share one thing from his letter with you. Then pray for each other. Ask God to help you implement your plan.

Lesson Planning (55-80 minutes)

Remember these four characteristics of an effective teacher during your lesson-planning time. Perhaps you will be able to implement a portion of your letter during your planning time. You will be working on planning and preparing well.

Begin your planning time by praying together, asking God to help you be compassionate towards each other and the children. Pray for each other's needs. Pray for the needs of your learners. Ask God to continue to use your efforts to help your learners grow in compassion.

Plan all segments of the next several lessons that you will need to complete together. Be sure each staff member is clear on responsibilities for each session. Help each other with ideas. Share materials. Share ideas for helping learners apply Scripture to their lives.

Training Sessions

BECOMING AN EFFECTIVE TEACHER

G _ _ w _
s _ _ r _ _ _ _ l _ _
and in c h _ _ _ c _ _ r
On a scale of 1-10, I rate _____.

P _ a _ _ _   and
p _ e _ _ _ _ _
w _ _ _
On a scale of 1-10, I rate _____.

B _ _ _ _ _ _
r _ l _ _ i o _ _ _ _ _ _
On a scale of 1-10, I rate
_____.

H _ _ _ _
l _ _ r _ e _ _
a _ p _ _
S _ _ _ _ t _ _ _
On a scale of 1-10, I rate _____.

BUILDING RELATIONSHIPS
(1 ½–2 hours)

Aims
During this training session, each participant may
- Explore the importance of developing a caring relationship with each learner.
- Apply a biblical model for a caring relationship to the teaching situation today.
- List actions that will lead to a caring relationship.
- Prepare a card for each learner that will record aspects of the relationship-building process.
- **Option:** Identify the integration of the character virtue compassion.

Materials
Bibles	Large index cards
Lesson planning sheets	Scissors
Curriculum	Glue
Photocopies of page 90	Markers
Magazines	Pencils
Large sheets of shelf paper or newsprint	Chalkboard and chalk or poster board

Preparation
1. Ask participants to bring their Bibles, their curriculum, and their class lists with all available information about the learners.

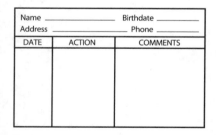

2. Prepare index cards according to the sketch. Each teacher needs one for every learner plus five or six extras for children who may join the class.

3. Photocopy page 90 for each participant.

4. Bundle each teacher's cards with rubber bands. Put teachers' names on the correct bundles.

5. Place large sheets of paper at tables or on the floor. Six to eight participants can work as one group. Put markers, magazine pictures, scissors, and glue at each location.

6. **Option:** Display the word *compassion*.

Arrival Activities (arrival plus 3-5 minutes)
1. Have participants find magazine pictures that illustrate the building of compassionate and caring relationships. Instruct each group to create a collage on their large paper. They may use markers to add words or phrases.

2. Ask participants to locate their bundles of cards. Explain how to use the cards. If time permits, they may begin to fill in learner information at the top of each card.

Exploration Activities (15-20 minutes)

Ask participants to sit in groups of four to six. Each group needs several Bibles. Explain that for five to ten minutes, participants are to explore a Biblical example of compassionate and caring relationships.

One goal of our teaching is changed lives. God's Word does change lives. If it is shared in an atmosphere of compassionate, caring relationships, lives are enriched, and both learners and teachers are encouraged.

Direct half of the groups to read Mark 10:13-16 and the other half to read Matthew 19:13, 14. Ask each group to discuss these questions:

• How did Jesus model the relationship-building process? (He took time, touched, gave instruction, encouraged, modeled the concepts he was teaching.)

• What do you think about the time involved in building relationships? (Need to plan for it; evaluate priorities; recognize that building relationships is part of a teaching ministry.)

• How do relationships affect lives? (Compassionate, concerned relationships help build a sense of belonging, worth, and competence; provide understanding of needs, interests, and abilities.)

Brainstorm ways to build relationships. Ask someone in your group to jot down your group's ideas. Make a list that you can share with the rest of us. *Provide three to five minutes for brainstorming. As each group shares their ideas, these suggestions probably will be mentioned: use eye contact; be a good listener; smile; use children's names; touch; participate in special activities; send mail; make phone calls; attend sports and other special activities; mail birthday cards; visit in homes; plan group activities outside of class time; use in-class activities that require teamwork. Have the participants write the ideas on their response sheets.*

Response and Application (10-20 minutes)

Ask each participant to look at the list of ways to build relationships. Check at least three items you will work on with your students in the next month.

Continue to work on preparing individual cards for your learners. Fill in the basic information for all learners, and then write an idea for an activity in the "action" column for several of your learners. When this activity actually occurs, fill in the date and any comments.

Close your time together by making a commitment to begin and maintain a card for every learner in your classes. Pray that God will guide you to be able to invest time and to plan a meaningful "action" for every learner. Set a goal to complete the initial work on your cards during the next week. Then go through the cards each week as part of your individual planning time. Continue to initiate actions to demonstrate care, concern, and compassion for each learner.

Lesson Planning (40-70 minutes)

For the remaining time, work in teaching teams. Use Bibles, curriculum, and planning sheets to help make specific plans. Remember to integrate a Christian virtue in each lesson.

BUILDING RELATIONSHIPS

Read Mark 10:13-16 or Matthew 19:13, 14.
- How did Jesus model the relationship-building process?
- What do you think about the time involved in building relationships?
- How do relationships affect lives?

Ways to Build Relationships

❑ _____

❑ _____

❑ _____

❑ _____

❑ _____

❑ _____

❑ _____

❑ _____

❑ _____

❑ _____

❑ _____

BIBLE LEARNING ACTIVITIES FOR AGES 2-5

(1 ½–2 hours)

Aims

During this training session, each participant may
- Identify seven kinds of Bible learning activities that are appropriate for ages 2-5.
- Discover criteria for selecting Bible learning activities for a specific lesson.
- Experience several Bible learning activities.
- Plan effective conversation to use with a Bible learning activity for an upcoming lesson.
- **Option:** Identify the integration of the character virtue *initiative*.

Materials

Bibles
Lesson planning sheets
Curriculum
Overhead transparencies or poster board
Name tags (if needed)
Overhead projector (optional)
Photocopies of page 95
Transparency pens or markers
Pencils and paper
Index cards
Materials for simulated Bible learning activities

Preparation

1. Make photocopies of lesson planning sheets and page 95.
2. Prepare a poster or transparency of page 95.
3. Remind workers to bring their curriculum.
4. Gather and prepare materials for the Bible learning activities you plan to provide for this session. See pages 93 and 94 for descriptions of each activity. Prepare direction cards for each of the activities.
5. Arrange the materials for each activity in different places around the room.
6. Print the following directions for arrival activities on a poster or transparency:
   - Read Genesis 1:1–2 9.
   - List activities you have used to teach portions of this Scripture to young children.
   - Place a happy face beside activities you listed that involved the learners.
   - Put an "X" beside methods in which the learners were passive.
7. **Option:** Display the word *initiative*.

Arrival Activities (arrival plus 3-5 minutes)

1. Have each person put on a name tag if they are needed to help people become better acquainted.

2. Call attention to the arrival activity directions, that you printed on a poster or transparency. Briefly discuss the arrival activity results.

Exploration Activities (20-30 minutes)

Distribute photocopies of the response sheet. Display the poster or transparency you prepared to match.

Bible learning activities are activities designed to involve learners directly with Bible truth, helping to build initiative as children make important discoveries. Well-planned activities allow children to experience Bible concepts instead of just hearing about them. They make it possible to accomplish the aims of the session.

Carefully planned and prepared Bible learning activities correspond with the Bible content or application of the lesson. In addition, you will want to use activities that are appropriate for the age of your learners, manageable in your classroom, and teacher friendly.

Today we are going to discover seven kinds of Bible learning activities. Please use your response sheets to take notes about how to use each type of activity effectively. *Call attention to the activities you set up for workers to participate in later in the session. Walk to these areas as you talk about that particular kind of learning activity.*

Family living. If you can choose only one learning activity for very young children, please choose family living. The young child "plays out" activities from his daily life. Application of Bible concepts can be easily made through activities that are meaningful and taught in this familiar setting. If your classroom doesn't have special equipment for a family-living center, use any classroom table or a designated floor area.

Pictures and Books. A book or a picture related to the Bible story is an appropriate addition to any learning activity. Provide pictures and books related to both the Bible content and the application of a character virtue appropriate to the lesson. An open Bible with a story picture at the page where the Bible story is located is an effective addition to this area. Guide children to look at and talk about the pictures and the illustrations. Read the books as interest permits.

Nature. Children are fascinated by nature. As young children experience the wonder of God's creation, they develop awareness of the greatness of God. The five senses are used effectively as children explore nature items.

Art. The process is much more important than the finished product. Be sure the activity is age-appropriate. Younger children have limited small-muscle control. Conversation during the activity is the key factor in enabling the child to have a meaningful learning experience: "Thomas, the way you are using the color blue is a good idea. You sure can do good things on your own. That's called *initiative.*"

Blocks. Children can use blocks and accessory toys to learn many Biblical concepts. Younger children need cardboard or foam blocks. Fours and fives can use wooden blocks. Toddlers, twos, and threes will play side by side with blocks. Some fours and fives will discover that building cooperatively can be an enjoyable experience.

Games and puzzles. Be sure that games, puzzles, and other manipulative toys are safe and age-appropriate. Pieces that cannot be swallowed and puzzles with only a few pieces are appropriate for younger children.

Music. Music activities with young children include singing together during group time, listening to a recording, and using rhythm instruments. Action songs help to work out "wiggles." Bible words and character descriptions can be put to a familiar melody. Teachers can plan to sing spontaneously with one child or a small group of children when opportunity is there. Sometimes directions or greetings can be sung instead of spoken.

Response and Application (15-20 minutes)

Fortunately it is not necessary for us to devise Bible learning activities for every lesson. Begin with your curriculum. Read the activities suggested there and decide which ones to use as they are written. Adapt those that need some change in order to meet the needs of your learners and be effective in your situation. Sometimes you may wish to develop a new activity that will be especially meaningful to your learners.

Today I have prepared a variety of simulated Bible learning activities that could be used with a lesson from the Scripture you read as you arrived, Genesis 1:1–2:9. We will allow five minutes for each activity time. Each of you may choose to participate in three different activities. Follow the directions provided in each of the areas. Someone at each area needs to act as the teacher; the others in each group pretend to be children.

Conversation is the key to an effective Bible learning activity. Conversation with a teacher is what insures that Bible learning will take place. As you participate in an activity today, write on your response sheet some Bible words and questions you could use in conversation with children during that activity.

Before the session, prepare any or all of these or similar activities. Print the procedure to follow at each area on a large instruction card.

Family Living. Provide an assortment of fresh fruit and vegetables, plastic knife (for teacher's use), paper napkins, sponge for cleanup. Procedure: Look at the fruit and vegetables. Talk about the sizes, shapes, and colors. Smell the items. Cut the fruits and vegetables into bite-sized pieces and taste. Thank God for food. Talk about ways to give food to others.

Pictures and Books. Provide a Bible with a take-home paper picture of the Bible story placed at Genesis 1:1 and other books and pictures about things God created. Procedure: Read books and look at pictures. Talk about the things God made. Pray aloud to thank God.

Nature. Provide a Bible with a picture of something God made placed at Genesis 1:1, an assortment of things God created (leaf, apple, rock, shell, twig, etc.), and a magnifying glass (optional). Procedure: Read Genesis 1:1 from the Bible. Encourage children to handle, smell, and taste appropriate items and talk about the things God made. Talk about ways His creation makes us happy. Thank God for things He created.

Art. Provide a length of shelf paper, glue sticks, magazine pictures of things God created, and small nature items that can be glued to the collage. Procedure: Choose pictures and nature items to glue to the length of paper. Thank God for what he made.

Games and Puzzles. Provide a picture-matching game: Cut poster board into three-inch squares. Place one sticker of things God created on each square. Make two identical sets of squares. Procedure: Mix up squares; then place squares on a table or on the floor and match the pictures. Use two to four squares for twos, eight to ten for threes, and ten to twelve for fours and fives.

Lesson Planning (50-65 minutes)

Plan the next unit of lessons, giving special attention to the planning of Bible learning activities. Be sure each activity planned reinforces and/or helps to meet lesson aims, integrates Christian virtues, and allows teachers to use conversation, prayer, or Bible words and character descriptions effectively.

Training
Sessions

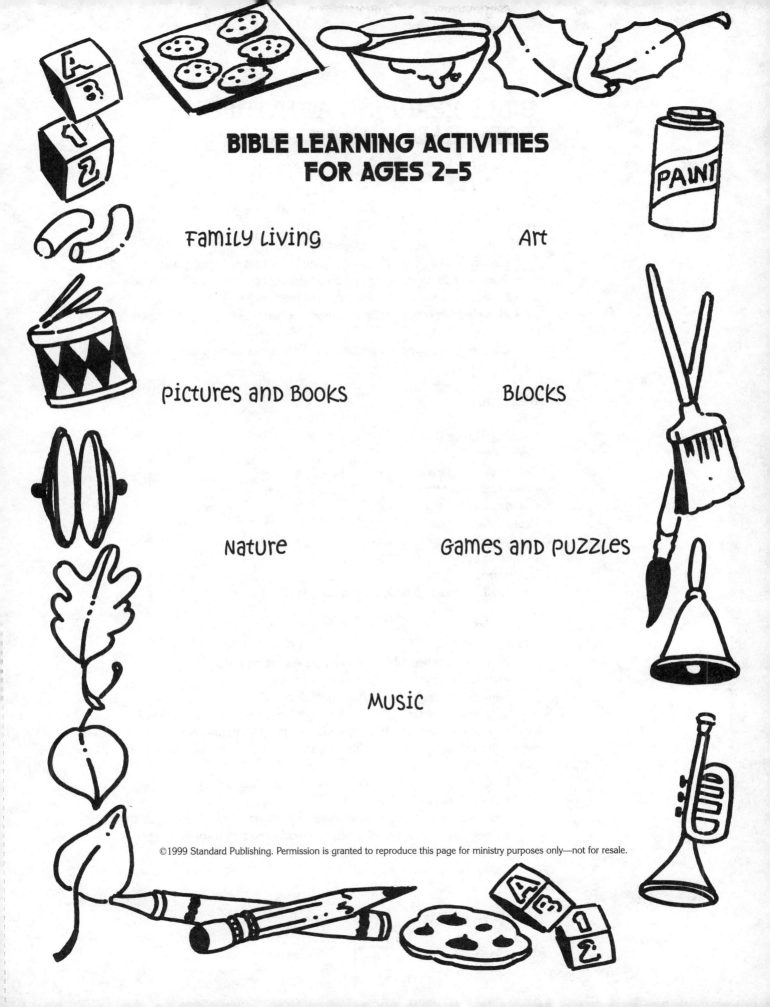

BIBLE LEARNING ACTIVITIES
FOR AGES 2-5

Family Living

Art

Pictures and Books

Blocks

Nature

Games and Puzzles

Music

BIBLE LEARNING ACTIVITIES FOR GRADES 1-6
(1 ½–2 hours)

Aims
During this training session, each participant may
- Identify five kinds of Bible learning activities that are appropriate for grades 1-6.
- Discover criteria for selecting Bible learning activities for a specific lesson.
- Experience several Bible learning activities.
- Plan effective conversation to use with a Bible learning activity for an upcoming lesson.
- **Option:** Identify the integration of the character virtue *initiative*.

Materials
Bibles
Lesson planning sheets
Curriculum
Overhead transparencies or poster board
Name tags (if needed)
Overhead projector (optional)
Photocopies of page 100
Transparency pens or markers
Pencils and paper
Index cards
Materials for simulated Bible learning activities

Preparation
1. Make photocopies of lesson planning sheets and page 100.
2. Photocopy page 100 onto a transparency.
3. Remind workers to bring their curriculum.
4. Gather and prepare materials for the Bible learning activities you plan to provide for this session. See page 99 for specific details. Prepare direction cards for each of the activities. Arrange the materials for each activity in different places around the room.
5. Print the following directions on a poster or transparency:
   - Read Genesis 1:1–2 9.
   - List activities you have used to teach portions of this Scripture to children.
   - Place a happy face beside activities you listed that involved the learners.
   - Put an "X" beside methods in which the learners were passive.
6. **Option:** Display the word *initiative*.

Arrival Activities (arrival plus 3-5 minutes)

1. Have everyone put on name tags if they are needed to help staff become better acquainted.

2. Ask participants to follow the directions on the poster or transparency you prepared.

3. Briefly discuss the arrival activity results.

Exploration Activities (20-30 minutes)

Distribute photocopies of page 100. Display the poster or transparency you prepared to match.

Bible learning activities are activities designed to involve learners directly with Bible truth, helping to build *initiative* as children make important discoveries. Carefully planned activities allow children to experience Bible concepts instead of just hearing about them. They make it possible to accomplish the aims of the session.

Carefully planned and prepared Bible learning activities relate to the Bible content or Bible application of the lesson. Use activities that are appropriate for the age of your learners, manageable in your classroom, and teacher friendly.

Every Bible learning activity needs to include three items:

• **Guided conversation.** It is the teacher's responsibility to plan questions and comments that will encourage learners to focus on Bible concepts and/or the application of Bible truth. This important part of planning and guiding the activity ensures the reinforcement and application of Bible truth. ("Megan, you are always coming up with good ideas. That shows real initiative!")

• **Variety in participation.** Children learn in several different ways. They have a wide variety of skills and interests. Bible learning activities that are carefully chosen and planned can provide the variety children need. Sometimes one activity will provide a variety of ways to participate. For example, fifth and sixth graders can work together to produce a newspaper about a Bible event. Some may write articles, some may choose to draw illustrations and cartoons, some may design the layout, and others may prefer to use research skills to gather information.

• **Opportunities for research.** Even first graders can begin to gather information needed to complete an activity. Research can be as simple as gaining information by looking at a picture or listening to a cassette. Older elementary children may begin to use Bible dictionaries and concordances.

Today we are going to think about six kinds of Bible learning activities. Please use your response sheets to take notes about how to use each type of activity effectively. *Point out the activities from several of these areas that you set up for workers to participate in later in the session. Walk to these areas as you talk about that particular kind of learning activity.*

Art. Children enjoy and can learn from a variety of art activities: murals, montages, collages, cartoon drawing, posters, and many others. The finished project is not as important as the learning that occurs through the process. Children may work individually or in small groups to complete an art project. Organize materials so that children may practice responsibility in cleaning up and putting away. When possible, provide a place for work to be displayed.

Bible games. Playing games can accomplish review of information as well as help children learn new information. Often games are used to encourage memorization of Bible verses. Use game formats that are familiar to children. They will enjoy such games as Bible Baseball, Bible Football, Concentration and other matching games, sorting games, and more. Your curriculum will suggest games from time to time, and there are many game books available in Christian bookstores. Games are also effective in defining and practicing character virtues.

Writing activities. Creative writing can be as simple as labeling a part of a child's drawing with one word or writing a simple story dictated by a child. Older children will enjoy writing a diary from the perspective of a Bible person. Producing a newspaper such as the 'Jerusalem Journal' or 'Bethlehem Banner' can provide meaningful learning experiences with lots of variety. Some children may be the staff photographers and draw illustrations for the paper. Others may interview people for a front-page story. The possibilities are almost endless.

Drama. Drama activities provide opportunities for children to demonstrate understanding of Scripture as well as application of Biblical concepts. Pantomime, spontaneous plays (with or without costumes), role-play, puppet plays, and many other possibilities make drama an exciting kind of Bible learning activity.

Verbal activities. Verbal activities are easy to develop for children. Almost all children enjoy talking! Bible learning activities encourage children to talk in meaningful ways, focused on Bible content and application of Biblical truth and Christian character development. TV interviews, monologues, brainstorming, and discussion are only a few of the possible activities involving talking.

Research. Children may use maps, Bible dictionaries, a concordance, pictures, and a wide variety of books to gather information. With this information, learners then can become active participants in lesson presentation.

Look now at the list of activities you made when you arrived. How many of them can be classified into these six categories? What other kinds of activities did you list?

Response and Application (15-20 minutes)

Fortunately it is not necessary for us to create Bible learning activities for every lesson. Begin with your curriculum. Read the activities suggested there and decide which ones to use as they are written. Adapt those that need some change in order to meet the needs of your learners and be effective in your situation. Be sure to integrate the character virtue you selected for the lesson. Sometimes you may wish to develop a new activity that will be especially meaningful to your learners.

Today I have prepared a variety of simulated Bible learning activities that could be used with a lesson from the Scripture you read as you arrived, Genesis 1:1–2:9. Five minutes is planned for each activity time. Each of you may choose to participate in three different activities. Please follow the directions provided in each of the areas. Someone at each area needs to act as the teacher; the others in each group pretend to be children.

Conversation is the key to an effective Bible learning activity. Conversation with a teacher is what insures that Bible learning and character development will take place. As you participate in an activity today, write on your response sheet some questions and comments you could use in conversation with learners during that activity.

Before the session, prepare any or all of these or similar activities. Print the procedure to follow at each area on a large instruction card.

Art. Provide pictures of things God created cut from magazines, 12- to 24-inch circles cut from butcher paper or newsprint, glue or tape, scissors, Bibles, small nature items (leaves, small rocks, bark, etc.). Procedure: Select pictures and/or items to glue to the circles, illustrating God's creation. Some learners may wish to draw and cut out items to be added. Encourage learners to select a variety of items. Talk about the wonder of God's creation, what creation tells us about God's character, and thank him for his wonderful gifts. Praise his creativity. If you wish, write a Bible verse at the top of the circle.

Writing. Provide Bibles, "diaries" made by folding and stapling paper, pens or pencils. Procedure: Learners read the Scripture and then imagine that they are present at the time of creation. They will write entries in their diaries to describe the events of each day of creation. Encourage them to describe their feelings about the events. Several learners may share one of their accounts until an entry for each of the seven days has been read.

Verbal. Provide Bibles, paper, pens or pencils, a "microphone" (optional). Procedure: Participants will review the Bible passage and decide as a group on five or six thought-provoking questions to ask Adam. Select two learners to ask and answer the questions as if a news person were conducting a "man on the street" interview with Adam. (In an actual class, the information would be shared with others in the class by presenting the interview. Be sure to praise children for their initiative.)

Bible games. Provide index cards and markers or crayons. Procedure: Participants will number seven index cards one through seven. Then on seven other index cards, participants will draw what was created on each day of creation. Have the learners play a game of Concentration by turning all fourteen cards upside down on a table and trying to match what was created on each day with the corresponding number.

Drama. Provide seven rolls of crepe paper streamers in various colors. Procedure: Assign seven participants or groups of participants a day of creation. Allow each individual or group to choose a roll of crepe paper. Have them figure out a way to depict their day of creation using the crepe paper for other learners to guess. One group could wave blue crepe paper to make waves like the ocean. One group could wrap the torso, arms, and head of a person with green crepe paper to depict a tree.

Research. Provide several books on creationism versus evolution. Procedure: Participants will prepare a defense of creation against basic theories of evolution.

Lesson Planning (50-65 minutes)

Plan the next unit of lessons, giving special attention to the planning of Bible learning activities. Be sure each activity planned reinforces and/or helps to meet lesson aims, integrates a character virtue, and allows teachers to use conversation about Bible words and character development effectively.

BIBLE LEARNING ACTIVITIES
FOR GRADES 1-6

Art

Drama

Writing activities

Verbal activities

Bible games

Research

HELPING CHILDREN LEARN TO PRAY
(1 ½–2 hours)

Aims
During this training session, each participant may
- Identify seven principles of prayer.
- Develop a step-by-step sequence for teaching children to pray.
- Learn songs to teach children about prayer.
- **Option:** Identify the integration of the character virtues *compassion* and *forgiveness.*

Materials
Bibles
Lesson planning sheets
Curriculum
Overhead transparencies or poster board
Overhead projector (optional)
Photocopies of page 104
Transparency pens or markers
Stationery
Index cards

Preparation
1. Invite workers. Remind them to bring Bibles and curriculum. Suggest that reading curriculum materials prior to the meeting will facilitate an efficient lesson planning segment.

2. Make photocopies of lesson planning sheets and page 104. Prepare a transparency or poster of the response sheet.

3. Letter each of the following Scripture references on separate index cards:
Psalm 106:1; Psalm 109:26; Psalm 135:5; 1 John 1:9; 1 John 4:19.

4. Locate and learn several children's prayer songs in the music resources (cassette or CD) that come with your curriculum. Select songs that will be easy for your staff to use with children, songs that affirm God's love for the child, that praise God, and that express thanks to Him.

5. **Option:** Display the words *compassion* and *forgiveness.*

Arrival Activities (arrival plus 3-5 minutes)
1. Give Scripture cards to five people as they arrive. Ask them to be prepared to read the Scripture aloud.

2. Ask participants to sit in class or department groups and talk about the first time they can remember praying.

Exploration Activities (20 minutes)

"We are going to begin by identifying seven prayer principles. *Display poster or overhead transparency of the response sheet.* On your "Prayer Principles" worksheet (page 101), there is space for you to take notes about each principle.

Principle 1. Prayer is "caught" more than taught. The example of teachers and parents is far more powerful in teaching prayer than anything else. As children observe others praying comfortably, they will become more and more comfortable and willing to participate in prayer. Demonstrate that prayer is a natural and spontaneous part of life. Communicate that it is something you like to do. Lead children to experience a variety of times, places, and methods for prayer. Adult prayers can teach children that prayer is difficult and boring. Guard against this happening. *Teach/sing a prayer song about God's love for the child.*

Principle 2. Prayer brings real benefits and meets real needs. Children must feel a need to pray and must see the benefits of prayer. Why do we need to pray? *Record responses on a transparency, poster, or chalkboard. Include the ideas that God commands us to pray; prayer draws us closer to God; prayer communicates our desires and feelings to God; prayer lets us receive forgiveness and forgive others.*

Principle 3. Pray in words and sentences a child might use. Children think in concrete terms. Avoid symbolism and phrases that are not familiar to children, such as "We come before thy throne" and "Keep us under your wing." Take a sheet of stationery and at the top write "Dear God," as if you were writing a letter to God. Work together in groups of four to six to write a prayer in words that are appropriate for the age level that most of your group teaches. *After several minutes, allow two to three minutes for groups to share their prayers aloud.*

Principle 4. Prayer objectives need to fit the one praying. Help children to have prayer objectives that are their size. It is unrealistic to expect children to pray for the conversion of all the Muslims in the world when they are fearful of inviting a friend to Sunday school. Encourage them to choose prayer objectives within the scope of their ability to understand, such as, "God, please help me forgive my friend," or "God, please take care of Mr. and Mrs. Jones, who live in India."

Principle 5. Prayer requests and results need to be visualized. Encourage children to bring photographs of their family and friends for whom they wish to pray. Make a chart to help children list what they are praying about, the date they begin to pray, the date God answered, and how He answered.

Principle 6. Prayer may be answered differently than expected. God's answer may be "yes," "no," "wait," or "Here's something better." Children need to know that prayer is not a magical way of getting everything they want. Life is immediate for children. It is difficult for them to see beyond the present need or desire. Prayer is a way of building trust in God. It will help children begin to know God and to build a friendship with him.

Training Sessions

Principle 7. Prayer is learned more effectively when experienced step by step.
Ask the five participants who prepared Scripture verses to read them aloud one at a time, in the following order. Discuss each one.

Psalm 136:5 tells us something about who God is. When we get to know who God is and how much he loves us, our response is to love him in return. Here is a song that helps children know more about God. *Teach/sing a praise song from your curriculum resources.*

1 John 4:19 tells us we can say "I love you" to God. Adoration and praise need to be elements in all prayers. A love for God expressed in a child's earliest prayers helps to develop a pattern of compassion, love, and care that will continue throughout life.

Psalm 106:1 tells us to give thanks to God. This prayer concept is related to the natural inclination and parental teaching to be thankful for things given to us. Who gives us everything? God does. Children can simply say, "Thank you, God." *Teach/sing a song expressing thanks.*

Psalm 109:26 tells us it is good to ask God for help. As children become comfortable in telling God they love him, in thanking God for things and asking his help in their own lives, broaden their prayers to include praying for others' needs as well.

1 John 1:9 teaches us to confess our sins to God and to thank him for forgiving us. At an early age children realize that their actions are sometimes displeasing to parents and other significant adults in their lives. Telling others and God is the first step to making things right. Thanking God for forgiving us strengthens the belief that God does forgive.

Response and Application (5-10 minutes)
Ask each group to select at least one song or activity to use with their learners during the next several weeks. End by singing together one of the songs you began to learn earlier.

Lesson Planning (45-75 minutes)
Dismiss class/department groups to begin to plan for the next month or unit of lessons. Ask them to begin by praying for one another and for their learners, keeping in mind the seven prayer principles. Include specific planning to implement the prayer principles that have been shared.

PRAYER PRINCIPLES

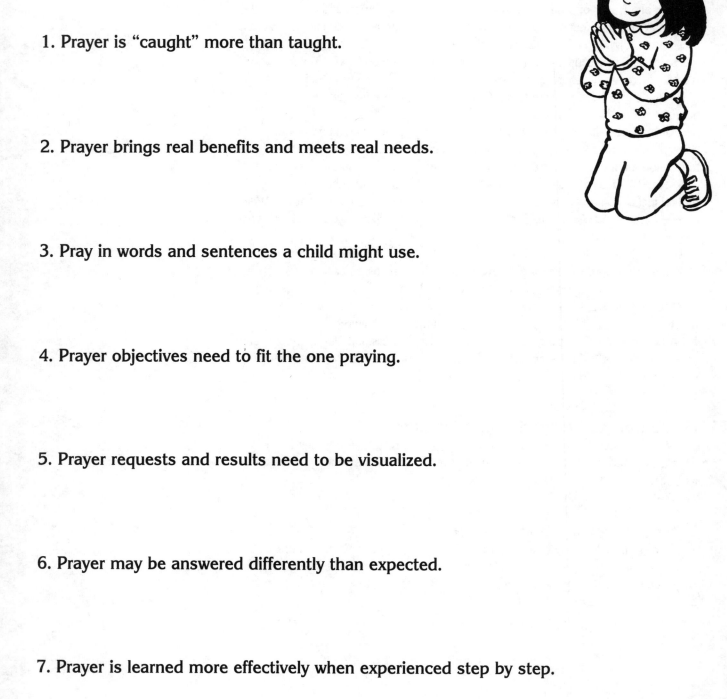

1. Prayer is "caught" more than taught.

2. Prayer brings real benefits and meets real needs.

3. Pray in words and sentences a child might use.

4. Prayer objectives need to fit the one praying.

5. Prayer requests and results need to be visualized.

6. Prayer may be answered differently than expected.

7. Prayer is learned more effectively when experienced step by step.

HELPING CHILDREN MEMORIZE SCRIPTURE
(1 ½–2 hours)

Aims

During this training session, each participant may

- Discuss reasons for helping children memorize Scripture.
- Experience a variety of ways to help children memorize Scripture.
- Select a method and/or a game to use during the next unit.
- Begin to memorize the verse or passage learners will be memorizing during the next unit.
- **Option:** Identify the integration of the character virtue *integrity*.

Materials

Bibles
Bible-memory games and other resources
Curriculum
Overhead transparencies or poster board
Lesson planning sheets
Overhead projector (optional)
Transparency pens or markers
Photocopies of page 108

Preparation

1. Remind workers to bring their Bibles and curriculum.
2. Make photocopies of lesson planning sheets and page 108.
3. Write these two questions on a poster or transparency:
   - Why is it important to help children memorize Scripture?
   - What is one effective method you have used?
4. Gather and prepare Bible-memory games and other resources.
5. Place name tags near the door if participants need them to become better acquainted.
6. **Option:** Display the character word *integrity*.

Arrival Activities (arrival plus 3-5 minutes)

1. Ask participants to think about the two questions on the poster or transparency:
   - Why is it important to help children memorize Scripture?
   - What is one effective method you have used?
2. After a short thinking time, ask participants to form groups of two or three and discuss their answers.
3. Ask participants to regroup and sit with others who teach the same age level.

Exploration Activities (15-20 minutes)

Let's share some of the reasons it is important for us to help children memorize Scripture. *Ask two or three people to share the responses they gave earlier.* Six important reasons are given in Scripture itself. *You may wish to have these written on a poster or transparency. Reveal each one as you read and discuss each verse. Have participants record their observations on the response sheet.*

Hebrews 4:12 tells us that memorizing Scripture will lead to conviction.

Psalm 119:11 tells us that memorizing Scripture will help us resist temptation.

Romans 15:4 tells us that Scripture can be a comfort in difficult times.

Psalm 119:105 tells us that Scripture is our guide to knowing God's plan for living.

1 Peter 3:15 tells us that memorized Scripture can be used as a means of sharing our faith with others.

John 17:17 tells us that Scripture is God's truth and that helps us become people of integrity.

Let's look at five ways to make Scripture memorization more effective. *You may wish to have these five ways written on a poster or transparency. Reveal each one as it is discussed. Participants can make notes on their response sheets.*

First, **model memorization by memorizing the same verse or passage that your learners are memorizing.** Your curriculum will suggest verses that relate to or reinforce the Bible content being taught. Take the opportunity to increase the verses you can quote by memorizing with your learners.

Second, **select a method of teaching that enhances the meaning of the verse or passage.** For example, if a verse asks a question, letter it on a cutout question mark. Or write a verse on the back of a picture that illustrates application of that verse.

Third, **use a variety of methods.** An effective method that is overused becomes less and less effective. Many resources are available with suggestions for activities and games that encourage memorization. Begin with the ideas in your curriculum. *Display some of the resources you have gathered. Tell how participants may share, check out, or purchase resources that interest them.*

Fourth, **share your excitement for Bible memorization.** Learners will get excited if you are excited.

Last, **have faith that God will use his Word in the lives of the learners who are memorizing it.**

Response Activities (10-15 minutes)

Display around the room the resources and Bible-memory games you have gathered and prepared. During the next 10-15 minutes, investigate the Bible-memory games and other materials that you see on display around the room. Select at least one game or activity that you know will be effective in your class. Think about the interests of your learners and the learning skills they can use.

Lesson Planning (50-80 minutes)

Work in teaching teams to plan the lessons for the next unit. During this planning time, focus on methods to encourage memory work. Try to use a variety of methods.

Plan for ways to help learners understand and apply the verses or passages they will be learning. Plan ways to demonstrate and discuss how the verse they are learning helps them know what is true and how that truth can help them become people of integrity.

Bible Memory Games

Here are several examples of Bible-memory games you may wish to provide for this training session. Also provide the materials necessary for making the games and encourage workers to take materials home with them to make games for their own classes. Display additional activities, games, and other materials available to you.

Toss the Beanbag. Learners stand or sit in a circle. Toss a beanbag or a foam ball back and forth. As each learner catches the beanbag, he says the next word in the verse. Younger learners will prefer to sit in a circle on the floor and roll the ball.

String-a-Verse. On poster board, randomly write the words and reference of a verse. Place a paper fastener in front of each word. Tie a piece of yarn around the fastener at the first word of the verse. Learners loop the yarn around the fasteners to show the correct sequence. Check answers with a Bible or answer card.

Bible-Verse Scramble. Write the words and reference of a verse on index cards, one word to a card. Mix up the cards. Place them in an envelope on which you have written the verse and reference. Learners remove the cards, arrange them in the correct order, and check their answer with the envelope or their Bibles.

Match the Shape. Cut simple shapes out of poster board, one shape for each word of a verse. Glue the piece with the shaped cutout to another piece of poster board the same size. Write the words of the verse on the cutout shapes, one word per shape. Learners put the verse together in sequence by matching shapes.

HELPING CHILDREN MEMORIZE SCRIPTURE

Six important reasons to help children memorize Scripture:

Hebrews 4:12

Psalm 119:11

Romans 15:4

Psalm 119:105

1 Peter 3:15

John 17:17

Ways to make Scripture memorization more effective:

1. Model memorization by memorizing yourself.

2. Select a method that enhances the meaning of the verse.

3. Use a variety of methods.

4. Share your excitement for memorization.

5. Have faith that God will use his Word in the lives of the learners.

FAMILY MINISTRY: BUILDING A BRIDGE BETWEEN CHURCH AND HOME
(1 ½–2 Hours)

Aims
During this training session, each participant may
- Identify existing relationships between the church and the families of learners.
- Recognize needs of families.
- Discover the "Five Ns" needed in order to build bridges between the church and home.
- Plan to implement one or more of the "Five Ns."
- **Option:** Identify the integration of the character virtue *cooperation*.

Materials
Bibles
Lesson planning sheets
Curriculum
Overhead transparencies or poster board
Name tags (if needed)
Overhead projector (optional)
Photocopies of page 112
Transparency pens or markers
Pencils
Index cards

Preparation
1. Make photocopies of page 112.
2. Prepare transparencies or posters of page 112 and these directions:
   - Read Deuteronomy 6:4-9.
   - Talk with two other people about the implications of these verses for both the church and the home.
3. Place name tags near the door if participants need them to become better acquainted.
4. **Option:** Display the word *cooperation*.

Arrival Activities (arrival plus 3-5 minutes)
1. Have participants wear name tags if needed for getting acquainted.
2. Display the transparency or poster you prepared with directions to read and talk about Deuteronomy 6:4-9.
3. Allow participants to discuss the verses.

Exploration Activities (15-20 minutes)

As you arrived, you were asked to read some verses from Deuteronomy. What are some of the implications of this passage for teaching as well as for parenting? *Encourage several participants to share. Record responses on a poster, transparency, or chalkboard.*

It is clear that the church has the responsibility of encouraging parents to be serious about their responsibility for Christian education. The church staff, both full-time and volunteer, may cooperate in prayer and planning.

Both spoken and written communications contribute to the overall effectiveness of relationships between church and home. In groups of three or four, brainstorm how church staff members can communicate with parents in both spoken and written ways. *After several minutes, have groups share their ideas. Record responses. Perhaps some participants would be willing to role-play some of the suggestions.*

Make your communication clear. Avoid complicated newsletters. Instead, put on one sheet all the necessary communication for the week. Some children may wish to decorate the sheet before taking it home. Occasionally you may wish to mail the information to each home. A phone call during the week does a lot to build positive relationships with all family members. Fax and e-mail are becoming increasingly popular means to reach people.

Part of the effort to communicate must be directed to the entire congregation. Nothing will substitute effectively for clear, current, and meaningful congregational awareness of what is going on in children's ministries.

In your groups, list ways your class or department could increase congregational awareness. *Again, have groups share their ideas. Record responses on a poster or transparency.*

Response and Application (20 minutes)

Display a transparency or poster listing the "Five Ns": Invest, Inform, Invite, Involve, and Encourage. Distribute the response sheets with space for making notes. Have participants work in department or class groups to discuss and respond to these questions:

1. What are some ways we can invest time in the homes of our children? *Shop or prepare a meal when mom is ill; watch children at times of family emergencies; call to express appreciation for an especially helpful behavior of a child; provide tutoring for children's homework.*

2. What are some specific things we can do to inform families about the programs at church for their children? *Send letters at the beginning of each new unit; place an insert in the bulletin; regularly place information in the church newsletter.*

3. How can we invite parents to participate? How can their participation help to increase parenting skills as well as a sense of cooperation within the church family? *Invite families to share with you at a church potluck meal; invite parents to visit class a few at a time; ask parents for input about classroom activities.*

4. How can parents be involved in church programs for their children? List a variety of ways, because not all parents are able to teach. *Ask parents to provide healthful snacks as needed or to help prepare materials for classroom use; give parents specific prayer needs and ask them to pray.*

Training Sessions

5. What can the church do to encourage parents? *Give parents photocopies of helpful articles; send notes of encouragement; recognize special events in families' lives, such as a new baby or a new home.*

Select at least one idea from one of the "Five Ns" to implement in your class or department. Pray together, asking God to enable you to find ways to cooperate with and minister to families.

Lesson Planning (50-70 minutes)

Plan the lessons in the next unit. Incorporate plans to minister to families. Invest some time in praying together. Share prayer concerns. Pray for individual learners and for needs of each family unit. Ask God for wisdom as you plan to minister to the families of your church's learners.

FAMILY MINISTRY: BUILDING A BRIDGE BETWEEN CHURCH AND HOME

Invest

What are some ways we can **invest** time in the homes of our children?

Inform

What are some specific things we can do to **inform** families about the programs at church for their children?

Invite

How can we **invite** parents to participate?

Involve

How can parents be **involved** in church programs for their children?

Encourage

What can the church do to **encourage** parents?

Select at least one idea from one of the "Five Ns" to implement in your class or department. What is it?